Strategic READING 2

Building Effective Reading Skills

Student's Book

CAMBRIDGE
UNIVERSITY PRESS

Jack C. Richards Samuela Eckstut-Didier

PUBLISHED BY THE PRESS SYNDICATE OF THE UNIVERSITY OF CAMBRIDGE
The Pitt Building, Trumpington Street, Cambridge, United Kingdom

CAMBRIDGE UNIVERSITY PRESS
The Edinburgh Building, Cambridge CB2 2RU, UK
40 West 20th Street, New York, NY 10011-4211, USA
10 Stamford Road, Oakleigh, VIC 3166, Australia
Ruiz de Alarcón 13, 28014 Madrid, Spain
Dock House, The Waterfront, Cape Town 8001, South Africa

http://www.cambridge.org

First published 2003

Printed in Hong Kong, China

Typeface Baskerville Book *System* QuarkXPress® [AH]

A catalog record for this book is available from the British Library

Library of Congress Cataloging in Publication data available

ISBN 0 521 555809 Student's Book 1
ISBN 0 521 555779 Teacher's Manual 1
ISBN 0 521 555795 Student's Book 2
ISBN 0 521 555760 Teacher's Manual 2
ISBN 0 521 555787 Student's Book 3
ISBN 0 521 555752 Teacher's Manual 3

Art direction, book design, and layout services: Adventure House, NYC

Contents

Authors' Acknowledgments **v**

Scope and sequence **vi**

Introduction **x**

UNIT 1 **Names** **1**
Naming traditions 2
Do people like their first names? 4
Changing maiden names 6

UNIT 2 **Games** **9**
Games for you to play 10
Majestic 12
Women playing games 14

UNIT 3 **Dance** **17**
Have fun with dance 18
Oriental dance: A dance for the whole family 20
Enjoying ballet 22

UNIT 4 **Helping others** **25**
If you see someone in trouble, don't just stand there 26
Random acts of kindness 28
Monkey business is Henrietta's middle name 30

UNIT 5 **Movies** **33**
Stunt school 34
Movie extras 36
The storyteller 38

UNIT 6 **Families** **41**
Living with mother 42
Father's Day 44
The incredible shrinking family 46

UNIT 7 **Men & women** **49**
The knight in shining armor 50
Men, women, and sports 52
Barefoot in the Park 54

UNIT 8 **Communication** 57
Spotting communication problems 58
Can babies talk? 60
Watch your language 62

UNIT 9 **Dishonesty** 65
The telltale signs of lying 66
If it sounds too good to be true . . . 68
Truth or consequences 70

UNIT 10 **Etiquette** 73
Cell phone yakkers need manners 74
How table manners became polite 76
Dinner with my parents 78

UNIT 11 **Love** 81
True love is over in 30 months 82
Choosing a dog is like falling in love 84
Love Song for Lucinda; Ashes of Life 86

UNIT 12 **Fear** 89
Flying? No fear 90
Don't fight a good fright 92
Fighting stage fright 94

UNIT 13 **The paranormal** 97
Using hypnosis to combat stress 98
Psychic solves crimes 100
What is a near-death experience (NDE)? 102

UNIT 14 **Languages** 105
The day a language died 106
Aping language 108
The bilingual brain 110

UNIT 15 **The senses** 113
Ice cream tester has sweet job 114
Primer on smell 116
How deafness makes it easier to hear 118

UNIT 16 **Heroes** 121
What does it take to be a hero? 122
Are athletes worthy heroes? 124
The hero of my life 126

Acknowledgments 129

Authors' Acknowledgments

The publisher would like to thank the following **reviewers** for their helpful insights and suggestions: Orlando Carranza, Ann Conable, Elliot Judd, Madeleine Kim, Laura LeDréan, Laura MacGregor, Sandy Soghikian, Colleen Weldele, and Junko Yamanaka.

We would also like to acknowledge the **students** and **teachers** in the following schools and institutes who piloted materials in the initial development stages:

Associação Alumni, São Paulo, Brazil; **AUA Language Center**, Bangkok, Thailand; **Case Western Reserve University**, Cleveland, Ohio, USA; **Hokusei Gakuen University**, Sapporo, Japan; **Hunter College**, New York, New York, USA; **Instituto Brasil-Estados Unidos (IBEU)**, Rio de Janeiro, Brazil; **Instituto Cultural Peruano Norteamericano**, Lima, Peru; **Kyung Hee University**, Seoul, Korea; **Miyagi Gakuin Women's College**, Miyagi, Japan; **Queens College**, Flushing, New York, USA; **Sapporo International University**, Sapporo, Japan.

We also would like to thank the many additional schools in the above countries whose students responded to surveys on their reading interests and preferences.

A special thanks to Lynn Bonesteel and Robert L. Maguire for their invaluable advice and support. The authors are also grateful to Chuck Sandy for his contribution to the early development of the project.

Thanks also go to the **editorial** and **production** team: Eleanor Barnes, Sylvia Bloch, David Bohlke, Karen Davy, Tünde Dewey, Anne Garrett, Deborah Goldblatt, Nada Gordon, Louisa Hellegers, Lise Minovitz, Bill Paulk, Mary Sandre, Howard Siegelman, Jane Sturtevant, and Louisa van Houten.

Finally, special thanks to Cambridge University Press **staff** and **advisors**: Jim Anderson, Mary Louise Baez, Carlos Barbisan, Kathleen Corley, Kate Cory-Wright, Riitta da Costa, Elizabeth Fuzikava, Steve Golden, Yuri Hara, Gareth Knight, Andy Martin, Nigel McQuitty, Mark O'Neil, Dan Schulte, Catherine Shih, Su-Wei Wang, and Ellen Zlotnick.

Scope and sequence

Unit	Readings	Skills	Vocabulary
Unit 1 **Names**	Naming traditions Do people like their first names? Changing maiden names	Guessing meaning from context Making inferences Predicting Recognizing audience Scanning Understanding details Understanding main ideas	Name-related terms
Unit 2 **Games**	Games for you to play Majestic Women playing games	Guessing meaning from context Predicting Recognizing point of view Recognizing sources Scanning Skimming Summarizing Understanding details	Game-related terms
Unit 3 **Dance**	Have fun with dance Oriental dance: A dance for the whole family Enjoying ballet	Guessing meaning from context Predicting Recognizing point of view Recognizing sources Restating Skimming Scanning Understanding details Understanding main ideas	Dance-related terms Phrasal verbs Compound nouns
Unit 4 **Helping others**	If you see someone in trouble, don't just stand there Random acts of kindness Monkey business is Henrietta's middle name	Predicting Recognizing purpose Recognizing similarity in meaning Scanning Understanding details Understanding main ideas	Phrasal verbs

Unit	Readings	Skills	Vocabulary
Unit 5 **Movies**	Stunt school Movie extras The storyteller	Guessing meaning from context Making inferences Predicting Recognizing sources Scanning Understanding details	People involved in movie-making Parts of a movie Types of movies
Unit 6 **Families**	Living with mother Father's Day The incredible shrinking family	Guessing meaning from context Predicting Scanning Summarizing Understanding details Understanding main ideas	Compound adjectives
Unit 7 **Men & women**	The knight in shining armor Men, women, and sports Barefoot in the Park	Guessing meaning from context Making inferences Predicting Scanning Skimming Understanding details Understanding figurative language Understanding reference words Understanding a sequence of events	Homonyms
Unit 8 **Communi-cation**	Spotting communication problems Can babies talk? Watch your language	Making inferences Predicting Recognizing audience Recognizing similarity in meaning Restating Scanning Skimming Understanding details Understanding reference words	Word formation

Unit	Readings	Skills	Vocabulary
Unit 9 **Dishonesty**	The telltale signs of lying If it sounds too good to be true . . . Truth or consequences	Guessing meaning from context Predicting Recognizing tone Scanning Understanding details Understanding reference words	Prefixes (*dis-*)
Unit 10 **Etiquette**	Cell phone yakkers need manners How table manners became polite Dinner with my parents	Guessing meaning from context Predicting Recognizing audience Restating and making inferences Scanning Skimming Summarizing Understanding details Understanding complex sentences	Suffixes (*-ful*)
Unit 11 **Love**	True love is over in 30 months Choosing a dog is like falling in love Love Song for Lucinda; Ashes of Life	Guessing meaning from context Predicting Recognizing audience Rhyming Scanning Understanding details Understanding main ideas	Love idioms Rhymes
Unit 12 **Fear**	Flying? No fear Don't fight a good fright Fighting stage fright	Guessing meaning from context Predicting Recognizing similarity in meaning Scanning Skimming Understanding details Understanding text organization	Fear-related words and expressions

Unit	Readings	Skills	Vocabulary
Unit 13 **The paranormal**	Using hypnosis to combat stress Psychic solves crimes What is a near-death experience (NDE)?	Guessing meaning from context Predicting Recognizing similarity in meaning Scanning Skimming Understanding details	Homonyms
Unit 14 **Languages**	The day a language died Aping language The bilingual brain	Predicting Restating Restating and making inferences Scanning Skimming Summarizing Understanding details Understanding main ideas	Prefixes (*bi-* and *uni-*)
Unit 15 **The senses**	Ice cream tester has sweet job Primer on smell How deafness makes it easier to hear	Guessing meaning from context Making inferences Predicting Scanning Skimming Understanding details Understanding reference words	Idiomatic expressions (with *hear*, *see*, *smell*, *taste*, *touch*)
Unit 16 **Heroes**	What does it take to be a hero? Are athletes worthy heroes? The hero of my life	Guessing meaning from context Making inferences Predicting Recognizing sources Restating Scanning Skimming Understanding main ideas	Suffixes (*-ity*, *-ness*, and *-ship*)

Introduction

Overview

Featuring adapted texts from a variety of authentic sources, including newspapers, magazines, books, and websites, the *Strategic Reading* series allows students to build essential reading skills while they examine important topics in their lives.

Strategic Reading 2 is designed to develop the reading, vocabulary-building, and critical thinking skills of young-adult and adult learners of English at an intermediate level.

Format

Each book in the *Strategic Reading* series contains 16 units divided into three readings on a particular theme. Every unit includes the sections described below:

Preview

The units begin with brief descriptions previewing the readings in the unit. These descriptions are accompanied by discussion questions designed to stimulate student interest and activate background knowledge on the theme.

This page also introduces some of the vocabulary found in the readings. These words and phrases are recycled throughout the unit to provide students with many opportunities to process and internalize new vocabulary.

Readings

Different genres of readings have been gathered from novels, plays, magazines, textbooks, websites, poetry, newspapers, and editorials to reflect realistically the varied nature of the written world. These texts increase gradually in length and difficulty as students progress through the book. A full page of challenging exercises, divided into the following three sets of activities, focuses students on each reading.

Before you read

This section encourages students to think more carefully about a specific area of the theme. When students make predictions based on their personal experiences, a valuable link between background knowledge and new information is formed.

Reading

One *Skimming* or *Scanning* activity accompanies every reading in the book. In this section, students must either skim or scan a passage to look for specific information or to confirm predictions made in the pre-reading activity. After, students are instructed to read the whole text.

After you read

The exercises in this section concentrate on the following reading skills (see the Scope and sequence chart on pages vi–ix) developed throughout the book:

- understanding main ideas and details;
- making inferences and guessing meaning from context;
- understanding the organization and cohesion of a text;
- recognizing an audience, source, tone, or point of view;
- distinguishing fact from opinion; and
- understanding complex sentences and the sequence of events.

In order to focus on multiple skills and accommodate different learning and teaching styles, a wide variety of task types are featured in these exercises. These task types include multiple choice, matching, true/false, and fill in the blank. These varied activities are designed to practice all aspects of a particular skill, and to maintain the interest of both students and teachers.

Each reading ends with an exercise called *Relating reading to personal experience* that allows students to use vocabulary introduced in the unit to share their thoughts, opinions, and experiences in writing or in discussions.

Wrap-up

Every unit ends with a one-page review section where students apply and expand their knowledge of unit vocabulary to complete a variety of fun and challenging word games and puzzles.

As a final activity, students work on a project or participate in a discussion related to the unit theme. Activities such as designing and conducting surveys, researching and presenting information, and interviewing others provide meaningful closure to the unit.

Strategic Reading 2 is accompanied by a Teacher's Manual that contains a model lesson plan, definitions of key vocabulary, comprehensive teaching suggestions, cultural notes, unit quizzes, and answers to activities and quizzes.

UNIT 1 Names

You are going to read three texts about names. First, answer the questions in the boxes.

READING 1

Naming traditions

This book excerpt explains how people around the world use first and last names. Find out about the confusion this can cause.

1. In your country, which is placed first — your family name or your given name?
2. How is a married woman usually addressed in your country?

READING 2

Do people like their first names?

This newspaper article describes how people feel about their first names and why names are important to people.

1. Are you happy with your name? Did you like it when you were younger?
2. Do you have a nickname? If so, what is it?

READING 3

Changing maiden names

These letters from a newspaper advice column reveal opinions on whether a woman should keep her maiden name after marriage.

1. In your country, does a wife take her husband's name?
2. Why do you think some wives want to keep their maiden names?

Vocabulary

To find out the meanings of the words in *italics*, work with another student, ask your teacher, or use a dictionary. Then check (✔) the statements that are true about you.

_____ 1. My name is easy to *mispronounce*.

_____ 2. I've never *made fun of* someone else's name.

_____ 3. Most people *call* me by my nickname.

_____ 4. I *address* my parents by their first names.

_____ 5. My name is quite *original*.

Naming traditions

1 When former American President Bill Clinton traveled to South Korea to visit with President Kim Young Sam, he repeatedly referred to the Korean president's wife as Mrs. Kim. While the South Korean officials were offended, the U.S. delegation was embarrassed.

2 In error, President Clinton's advisers assumed that Koreans have the same naming traditions as the Japanese. President Clinton had not been informed that, in Korea, wives retain their maiden names. President Kim Young Sam's wife was named Sohn Myong Suk. Therefore, her correct name was Mrs. Sohn. In Korea, the family name comes before the given name.

3 President Clinton arrived in Korea directly after leaving Japan and had not shifted cultural gears. His failure to follow Korean customs gave the impression that Korea was not as important to him as Japan.

4 In addition to Koreans, other Asian husbands and wives who do not share the same surnames include Cambodians, Chinese, Hmong, and Vietnamese. This practice often puzzles English-speaking teachers when interacting with a pupil's parents. They become confused about the student's correct last name. Also, the number of names a person has changes with the culture. Koreans and Chinese use three names; the Vietnamese can use up to four.

5 Placing the family name (or surname) first is common among a number of Asian cultures, for example, Vietnamese, Hmong, Cambodian, and Chinese. This reversal from the American system of placing the family name last often causes confusion.

6 Mexican naming customs differ as well. When a woman marries, she keeps her maiden name and adds her husband's name after the word *de* (of): After marrying Tino Martínez, María González becomes María González de Martínez. When children are born, the name order is as follows: given name, father's family name, mother's family name. Tino and María's child Anita is named Anita Martínez González. This affects how they fill out forms in the United States.

7 Mexican applicants usually write their mother's family name in the last-name slot. When requested to fill in a middle name, they generally write the father's family name. This conforms to the sequence used at home. Consequently, in the United States, Mexicans are addressed by the last name written — the family name of the mother. This is not the last name they would ordinarily use. Instead, they would rather be called by their father's family name. This often causes confusion.

8 Here are a few ways to avoid embarrassment or offense:

- Don't assume a married woman uses her husband's last name.
- Remember that in many Asian traditions, the order of first and last names is reversed.
- Keep in mind that in Latino traditions, males prefer to use their father's family name, which frequently is filled in on forms as the middle name.
- Ask which names a person would prefer to use. If the name is difficult to pronounce, admit it, and ask the person to help you say it correctly.

Adapted from *Multicultural Manners*.

Before you read

Predicting

Read the first paragraph on the opposite page. Then check (✔) the information you think you will read about in the text.

_____ 1. different naming traditions used by people around the world

_____ 2. different naming traditions in the United States

_____ 3. reasons why some people's names are hard to remember

_____ 4. what happens to a woman's name when she gets married

Reading

Scanning

Scan the text to check your predictions. Then read the whole text.

After you read

Recognizing audience

A **Who do you think the text was written for? Check (✔) the correct answer.**

_____ 1. people who are coming to the United States for the first time

_____ 2. people who are going to a non-English speaking country

_____ 3. Americans who are living in a foreign country

_____ 4. Americans who are living in the United States

Understanding details

B **Write the correct name.**

1. Lee Hyun Ju is from Korea. Her fiancé's name is An Ho Jae.
   What is her name now? Ms. or Miss ___*Lee*___.
   What is his name? Mr. _________.
   What will her name be after she marries? Ms. or Mrs. _________.
2. Tomoko Kato is from Japan. Her fiancé's name is Hideo Suzuki.
   What is her name now? Ms. or Miss _________.
   What is his name? Mr. _________.
   What will her name be after she marries? Ms. or Mrs. _________.
3. Guadalupe Gomez is from Mexico. Her fiancé's name is Emilio Rodríguez.
   What is her name now? Ms. or Miss _________.
   What is his name? Mr. _________.
   What will her name be after she marries? Ms. or Mrs. _________.

Relating reading to personal experience

C **Answer these questions.**

1. Who do you call by their first name? Who calls you by your first name? Who do you call only by their last name?
2. How would your name be different in the other countries mentioned in the reading?
3. What would you tell a foreign visitor about the naming traditions in your country?

Do people like their first names?

Most do — or eventually will

1 As a shy girl growing up, Delana Pence got a lot of teasing from other children. Her unusual first name didn't help matters. "People would mispronounce it or make fun of it," said Pence, 40. "I asked myself why my parents named me this. Why couldn't I be a Cindy or a Rhonda?" Life got easier in junior high school when someone – Pence can't remember who – started calling her Dee and the nickname stuck. "I have been called Dee ever since, except by my family, who has always called me Delana." In time, Pence came to terms with her name. "It's a pretty name, but it took me all these years to struggle with it and figure that out," she said.

2 Her change of heart doesn't surprise Cleveland Kent Evans, an associate professor of psychology at Bellevue University, who has studied given names for more than 20 years. "A great many people – more women than men – go through a period during their adolescence where they dislike their name as part of the general adolescent concern with identity and what other people think of them," he said. "But I think for most people these feelings subside by the time they are in their 30s." Most people, Evans and other psychologists say, go through life with a favorable view of their names.

Delana

Ember

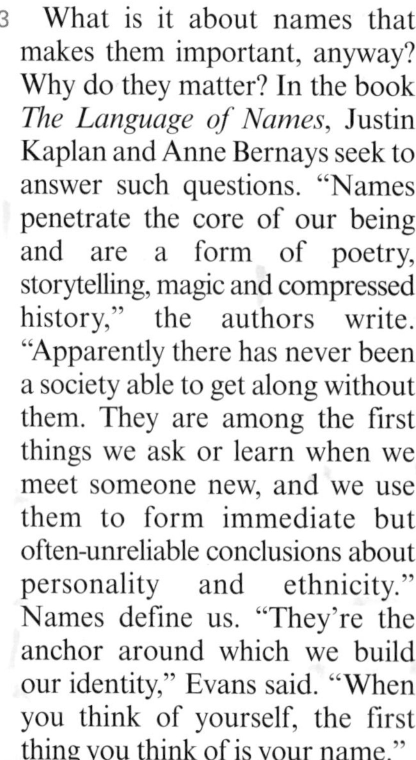

3 What is it about names that makes them important, anyway? Why do they matter? In the book *The Language of Names*, Justin Kaplan and Anne Bernays seek to answer such questions. "Names penetrate the core of our being and are a form of poetry, storytelling, magic and compressed history," the authors write. "Apparently there has never been a society able to get along without them. They are among the first things we ask or learn when we meet someone new, and we use them to form immediate but often-unreliable conclusions about personality and ethnicity." Names define us. "They're the anchor around which we build our identity," Evans said. "When you think of yourself, the first thing you think of is your name."

4 Nine-year-old Ember Gibson seems to be struggling with the identity issue, leaving her undecided about her name. "I get teased often, but then I have people compliment me too," Ember said. "Most of the kids call me Amber. Some say, 'Are you on fire?' And others say, 'What?' When I stop and think about it, though, I like that it's original. . . . Maybe by the time I graduate, I'll know if I like it or not."

READING TIP Scan the text to understand important details. Read quickly to look for information that answers a specific question, such as a number, name, word, or phrase.

Adapted from *The Columbus Dispatch*.

Predicting

Before you read

Look at the people in the pictures on the opposite page. Who do you think said each statement? Write Delana (*D*) or Ember (*E*).

I don't like my name. I wish I could change it.

1. E

I like my name. I think it's pretty.

2. D

I like my name now. But as a kid, it bothered me because it was unusual.

3. D

I like my name. It's different.

4. E

I'm not sure I like my name.

5. E

I don't like my name. Other kids make fun of it.

6. E

Scanning

Reading

Scan the text to check your predictions. Then read the whole text.

After you read

Understanding main ideas

A Write the number of the paragraph that each statement describes.

____ a. Names are very important to people.

____ b. Some children with unusual names dislike their names and use nicknames.

____ c. Most adults like their names, despite how they felt when they were younger.

Guessing meaning from context

B Find the words in *italics* in the reading. Then match each word with its meaning.

f	1. *stick* (par. 1)	a. the most important part
____	2. *come to terms* (par. 1)	b. become less and less
____	3. *change of heart* (par. 2)	c. a change of opinion
____	4. *subside* (par. 2)	d. accept a difficult situation
____	5. *favorable* (par. 2)	e. laugh at
____	6. *core* (par. 3)	f. continue or stay
____	7. *tease* (par. 4)	g. good

Relating reading to personal experience

C Answer these questions.

1. If you have a child, what would you name him or or her? Why? If you already have a child, what name did you choose? Why?
2. What are your three favorite English names for males? For females?
3. If you could change your name, what would you change it to? Why?

Changing maiden names

Between 1955 and 2002, Ann Landers' advice column appeared in more than 1,200 newspapers worldwide and helped millions of readers deal with everything from birth to death. The following are real letters that were written to Ann Landers.

Letter 1

Dear Ann,

Your advice to the woman who wrote "A Split Opinion in the Midwest" left a lot to be desired. She wanted to keep her maiden name after marriage. Her husband, however, insisted that she take *his* name. You suggested she compromise by using her maiden name professionally, and her husband's name socially.

I compromised by hyphenating our names when we married. It has made my husband happy, but I feel a little resentment every time I sign my name. Of course, it is too late to change back to my maiden name, because people will assume we are getting a divorce, so I have to live with my hyphenated name.

There are few things in life as personal as one's name. "Split's" fiancé should not ask her to do something he would not do himself. After all, she is the one who has to live with her choice, not him. A fiancé should make only those decisions regarding his name, and let his future wife do the same.

Mrs. BT-DT

Dear Mrs. BT-DT,

You are not the only one who thought my "compromise" was less than ideal. Here are some additional letters on the subject.

Ann

Letter 2

Dear Ann,

Your "compromise" won't work. Using two names will not last, and "Split's" name will be the one that disappears. I not only kept my own name, but with my husband's encouragement, our two daughters also have my last name. I admit it can be confusing sometimes, but in 16 years, I have never regretted my decision.

West Hartford

Letter 3

Dear Ann,

I changed my name because I believed it was silly to refuse when my fiancé and I loved each other so much. Ten years and one divorce later, I see it differently. His insistence on my name change was the first in a long list of things he did to control me. He told me how to wear my hair, what clothes to buy, what couples to spend time with, where to take our vacations, what time I was to wake up on the weekends, and how long I could talk on the phone to family members and friends. If her fiancé threatens not to marry her if she doesn't change her name, she should run as fast as she can in the opposite direction.

Kansas City

Letter 4

Dear Ann,

In 1964, I was madly in love. When I told my fiancé I wanted to keep my maiden name, he said, with tears in his eyes, "You don't love me." Hyphenating Di Napoli-Poffenberger was crazy, so I caved in. I cannot describe the feelings I had about disappearing as an individual. I did not receive class-reunion invitations, and my friends could not find my name in the phone book. Twenty-five years later, I told my husband I was going back to my maiden name and that he should know I loved him by now. It was difficult to change everything, and some of our friends asked if we were splitting up, but it was worth the hassle. Please tell that bride who wrote to stick to her guns.

San Diego

Adapted from *The Toronto Star.*

Before you read

Relating to the topic

Check (✔) the statements you agree with.

____ 1. After they marry, husband and wife should combine their names and use a hyphenated name (for example, Smith-Brown).

____ 2. When a woman takes her husband's name, it shows she loves him.

____ 3. A man who wants his wife to change her name is trying to control her.

____ 4. When a woman gives up her maiden name, she disappears as an individual.

Reading

Scanning

Scan the text to find out which statements the letter writers agree with. Then read all the letters.

After you read

Guessing meaning from context

A Find the words in *italics* in the reading. Circle the meaning of each word.

1. When you *compromise*, you accept something that is **the same as / a little different from** what you wanted at first. (Letter 1)
2. When you feel *resentment*, you feel **anger / happiness**. (Letter 1)
3. *Insistence* is saying something **doesn't have to / must** happen. (Letter 3)
4. If you *cave in*, you **agree / don't agree** to something you don't want to do. (Letter 4)
5. When people *split up*, they **separate / stay together**. (Letter 4)
6. When something is a *hassle*, it is **easy and nice / difficult and annoying**. (Letter 4)
7. If a woman *sticks to her guns*, she **changes / doesn't change** her opinion. (Letter 4)

Making inferences

B Match the questions and answers. (Be careful! There are two extra answers.)

____ 1. Why does Mrs. BT-DT feel a little resentment every time she signs her name?

____ 2. Why will "Split's" name be the one that disappears?

____ 3. Why was hyphenating Di Napoli-Poffenberger crazy?

____ 4. Why should San Diego's husband have known that she "loved him by now"?

____ 5. Why did San Diego's friends ask if she and her husband were splitting up?

a. She likes her husband's name.
b. Divorced women change names.
c. They've been married a long time.
d. She doesn't love her husband.
e. She never wanted to change her name.
f. It was difficult to say.
g. Children take the father's name.

Relating reading to personal experience

C Answer these questions.

1. What advice would you give to the writer of "A Split Opinion"? Why?
2. When children are older, should they be able to choose the family name they use? Why or why not?
3. Would you ever change your name? Why or why not?

Vocabulary expansion

Complete the crossword puzzle with words from the unit. The numbers in parentheses after the clues below show the reading in which the word appears.

Across

3. write your name in a particular way (1)
5. speak to someone using his or her name (2)
7. the name that comes between your first name and last name (1, 2 words)
8. another way to say "first name" (1, 2 words)
10. complete a form with your name and other information (1, 2 words)
11. put the mark (-) between two names (3)
14. speak to someone using his or her name (1)
15. say correctly (1)
16. give someone a name (2)

Down

1. a name used by someone's friends or family (2)
2. another way to say "last name" (1)
4. gave someone a name (1)
6. complete a form with your name and other information (1, 2 words)
7. a woman's last name before she marries (1, 2 words)
9. say incorrectly (2)
12. another way to say "last name" (1, 2 words)
13. who a person is (2)

Names and you

Work in groups. Make a list of all the first names in the class. Then make as many words in English as you can from the list. Which group makes the most words?

UNIT 2 Games

You are going to read three texts about games. First, answer the questions in the boxes.

READING 1

Games for you to play

Are you in the mood to play a game? This book suggests some games for you to try.

1. What was your favorite game when you were a child?
2. What kinds of games did you play inside on a rainy day? What about when you traveled somewhere by car or bus?

READING 2

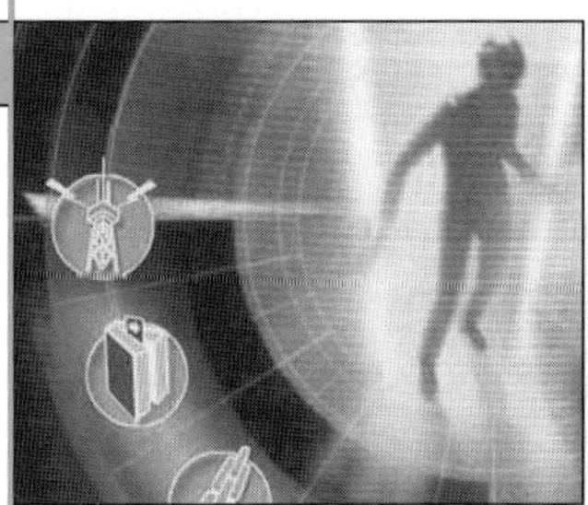

Majestic

Learn how to play a game that's part fantasy and part reality.

1. Do you play computer games? If so, which ones do you like? If not, why not?
2. Do you like games that involve figuring out a puzzle? Are you good at such games?

READING 3

Women playing games

Who enjoys playing video games more, men or women? Why? This newspaper article answers these questions.

1. What are some recent video games? What makes them popular?
2. Do you have a game console at home? If so, who uses it the most?

Vocabulary

Find out the meanings of the words in *italics*. Then check (✔) the statements that are true about you.

____ 1. Playing games is one of my favorite *pastimes*.

____ 2. I find new games very *appealing*.

____ 3. I don't mind playing a difficult game if it is *rewarding*.

____ 4. I enjoy games that allow me to *interact* with others.

____ 5. When I play a game with others, I like to *move into the lead* very quickly.

____ 6. When I play a game against others, I'm usually very *competitive*.

Games for you to play

1 Whether seven years old or 70, everyone enjoys a game. You may be all alone and bored or with a group of friends. You may have nothing to do on a rainy day but sit around and watch TV. Here is just a sampling of games for different ages and different moods.

Word lightning

2 The leader chooses a victim and gives him or her a letter. The unlucky victim then has sixty seconds in which to rattle off as many words as he or she can, beginning with the chosen letter. The leader keeps count. When all the players have been given a letter and a minute to do their best, the player with the highest word-count is the winner.

Boxes

3 Begin by drawing ten rows of ten dots so that the dots form the corners of a hundred little squares. Now players take turns connecting adjoining dots with straight lines going either vertically or horizontally. The object of the exercise is to be the player who completes the fourth side of a square, once the other three have been drawn. When players succeed in making a square, they mark it with their initials and get an extra turn. When all the squares have been completed and claimed, the player with the most squares is the champion.

Solo snap

4 All you have to do is turn over every single card in the deck while counting and not have any card come up as you call it. For example, as you turn over the first card, you say "Ace." If it is an Ace, the game's over and you've lost. If it is not, you continue. If something other than a two is the next card, all is well and on you go, until you have been through the Jack, Queen, and King, when you start all over again with the Ace. You win if you manage to turn over all fifty-two cards in the deck. Sounds simple, doesn't it? Well, it is almost impossible.

Kaleidoscope

5 All the players but one stand in a line facing the remaining player—let's call her Mary. In turn they tell her what "color" they are. (If there are six of them, they might be black, blue, red, pink, yellow, and turquoise.) Then they ask her to shut her eyes. While she has her eyes closed they all switch positions in line. When she reopens her eyes, she has to identify their original colors. Sounds simple? Try it and see.

Adapted from *Games for Rains, Planes, and Trains.*

Before you read

Predicting

Look at the pictures. Write the letters of the phrases you think refer to each picture.

1. ______ 2. ______ 3. ______ 4. ______

a. Ace, Jack, Queen, King
b. 100 little squares
c. as many words as possible
d. 52 cards in the deck
e. gives him a letter
f. keeps count
g. rows of ten dots
h. shut her eyes
i. stand in a line
j. switch positions
k. turn over
l. vertically or horizontally

Reading

Scanning

Scan the text to check your predictions. Then read the whole text.

After you read

Summarizing

A **Check (✔) the best summary of the text.**

____ 1. 100 outdoor games you can play
____ 2. game ideas for travel and home
____ 3. games for young children
____ 4. a brief history of games

Understanding details

B **Write the name of the game or games.**

1. You need to have a deck of cards to play this game. Solo snap
2. You have to have a good memory to win this game. K WL
3. You don't need any equipment to play this game. K WL
4. You can play this game when you are alone. Solo Snap
5. You have to be able to think fast to win this game. WL
6. You need to have luck to win this game. Solo Snap Boxes
7. This game is for more than two players. Kaleidoscope WL

Relating reading to personal experience

C **Answer these questions.**

1. Which game would you prefer to play? Why?
2. What are the best games to play when you're with a group of friends? What about when you're alone?
3. What are the rules of one of your favorite games?

Majestic

1 The message light on your phone is blinking. After you pick up, you hear the menacing voice of a strange man who warns you – by name – that you're in danger.

2 You've just entered the world of Majestic. Or, as the makers of the game like to say, it has just entered your world. But Majestic, an online computer game, isn't your average shoot-'em-up. Unlike most traditional video games, there is no digital, 3-D environment to navigate. Instead, the players themselves become pieces in the game's intricate web. They surf the Net, make and receive phone calls, e-mails, instant messages, and faxes, all in an effort to gather clues and unearth a terrible government conspiracy that plays out over a series of often-macabre episodes.

3 By jumping beyond the PC and using ordinary devices – something no modern game has done – Majestic makes a conscious effort to depart from the traditional video-game form and blur the line between fantasy and reality.

4 Majestic is geared for 18- to 35-year-olds – puzzle-loving women especially – who enjoy the fact that the game is designed to be played in 15-minute, not two-hour, chunks.

5 Neil Young, production chief at Electronic Arts, got the idea for Majestic in 1999, after hearing a panicked man call in to an Internet radio show that focuses on paranormal events. The man said that since he had recently left a top-secret military base, someone was chasing him. Just as he was about to reveal a key bit of information, the line went dead.

6 That's exactly the kind of thing that could happen in an anonymous audio or video file delivered into a Majestic player's e-mail account from EA's central servers.

7 "I couldn't tell whether (the phone call) was staged or whether it really happened – and that's Majestic," Young said. "We recreate the sense that you don't know what's real or not and you don't know what will happen next."

8 The Majestic pilot, which takes between three and five days to solve (three if you allow the game to call you at all hours of the night), will be available free via EA.com, the company's online hub. After that, consumers must pay about $10 to receive subsequent Majestic installments, which take about 12 to 15 days on average to complete.

Adapted from *The San Francisco Chronicle.*

Relating to the topic

Before you read

Check (✔) the games you would like to play.

____ 1. Play this word game and find the hidden words in a puzzle.

____ 2. Play this fantasy game and create a rich and happy island country.

____ 3. Play this money game and become the richest person in your town.

____ 4. Play this online game and become part of an intricate web of family relationships.

____ 5. Play this game online and navigate your way through the mystery.

____ 6. Play this shoot-'em-up game in a digital, 3-D environment.

Skimming

Reading

Skim the text to find out which game above the text describes. Then read the whole text.

After you read

Recognizing sources

A Where does the text probably come from? Check (✔) the correct answer.

____ 1. the Majestic website

____ 2. a women's magazine

____ 3. a newspaper article

____ 4. an advertisement

Guessing meaning from context

B Find the words in *italics* in the reading. Circle the meaning of each word or phrase.

1. When something is *menacing*, it can **help** / **hurt** you. (par. 1)
2. When you *unearth* something, you **discover** / **hide** it. (par. 2)
3. In a *conspiracy*, a small group secretly plans something **good** / **bad**. (par. 2)
4. When something is *macabre*, it is **fun and easy** / **strange and terrible**. (par. 2)
5. When you *blur the line*, you make the difference **clear** / **unclear**. (par. 3)
6. When people are *anonymous*, their names are **not known** / **well-known**. (par. 6)

Understanding details

C Find the answers to these questions in the text.

1. How is Majestic unlike traditional video games?
2. What is the goal for players of Majestic?
3. Who is Majestic intended for?
4. How much does it cost to play Majestic?

Relating reading to personal experience

D Answer these questions.

1. Would you like to play Majestic? Why or why not?
2. Are other games like Majestic popular today? Why or why not?
3. What kinds of computer or video games would you like someone to develop?

Women playing games

1 New video games are coming out all the time, with millions of titles on the market. In all this success, however, women are left on the sidelines.

2 According to industry estimates, around 20–30 percent of game players are women. Figures quoted by Internet-based communities of female players are even more bullish, suggesting that there is only a 7–15 percent margin between the sexes. But these figures are open to question.

3 Of course, if you look at sales statistics, women may buy as many game consoles and game titles as men, but they are often buying for others. How many actually play the games?

4 Moreover, the women that *do* play these games tend to do so as adjuncts to their male companions; they rarely touch the controls and are usually relegated to the role of advisor or watcher. The conclusion seems obvious: relatively few women play, discuss, or enjoy video games.

5 There are two main reasons for this. First, there is a widespread belief that the male-dominated video game world is a waste of time, and therefore of little social importance.

6 Second, the way that games are typically structured is not appealing to many women and the industry makes little effort to overcome this. In a business now thought to be worth more than movies, women are seldom involved in production and marketing.

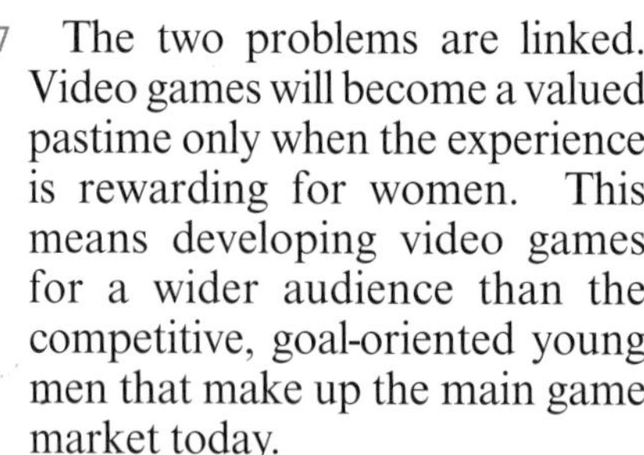

7 The two problems are linked. Video games will become a valued pastime only when the experience is rewarding for women. This means developing video games for a wider audience than the competitive, goal-oriented young men that make up the main game market today.

8 These values, around which most computer games are structured, have limited appeal to large numbers of women. If games could generate conversation and chat, were driven by choices, dilemmas, morality, and scruples, and allowed for players to interact and share, I believe women would be as captivated by the experience as men are now.

9 So far, developing games by men for men has served to keep the entire industry a large men's club that has succeeded by ignoring half the population.

READING TIP Knowing one word can help you guess the meaning of related words. For example, if you know the meaning of *market*, you can guess that *on the market* means "available for sale," *to market* means "to make products attractive to buyers," and *marketing* means "advertising."

Adapted from *Financial Times.*

Before you read

Relating to the topic

Check (✔) the column you agree with.

	Men	Women	Both
1. They buy game consoles.			
2. They buy video games.			
3. They usually buy game consoles and video games for others.			
4. When video games are played, they usually advise or watch.			
5. They prefer competitive, goal-oriented games.			
6. They prefer games that generate conversation and chat.			
7. They prefer games that involve dilemmas, morality, and scruples.			

Reading

Scanning

Scan the text to check your answers. Then read the whole text.

After you read

Guessing meaning from context

A **Find the words in *italics* in the reading. Then match each word with its meaning.**

c	1. *left on the sidelines* (par. 1)	a. not certain
____	2. *bullish* (par. 2)	b. very interested
____	3. *margin* (par. 2)	c. not participating in an activity
____	4. *open to question* (par. 2)	d. given a less important position
____	5. *adjuncts* (par. 4)	e. difference
____	6. *relegated* (par. 4)	f. less important people
____	7. *captivated* (par. 8)	g. expected to rise

Recognizing point of view

B **Check (✔) the statement that best describes the writer's opinion.**

____ 1. The video games on the market are very successful, so companies shouldn't change the type of games they are producing.

____ 2. Companies should change the type of video games they are producing, but the writer isn't sure how.

____ 3. Companies should stop producing video games for men and produce them for women.

____ 4. Companies should produce more video games that women would enjoy.

Relating reading to personal experience

C **Answer these questions.**

1. Do you know any games that involve choices, dilemmas, or scruples? What are they?
2. What video game do you like to play? Do both men and women enjoy it? Why or why not?
3. Do you think men and women prefer different games or only video games?

Vocabulary expansion

Check (✔) the correct column. (Note: In some cases, you can check both columns.)

	Rules of the game	Things people say during the game
1. Follow these rules.	✓	
2. Go back three spaces.		
3. If you land on an empty space, you miss a turn.		
4. It's not your turn. It's my turn.		
5. Roll the dice.		
6. Skip a space.		
7. Take turns.		
8. That's against the rules.		
9. That's my piece.		
10. Whose turn is it?		

Games and you

Create a board game in small groups. Decide the following:

1. What will the game practice — conversation, grammar, new vocabulary, spelling, or something else?
2. Will some of the squares remain blank? If so, how many?
3. What will go on the squares?
4. How many people can play the game at one time?
5. How do players win the game?
6. What are the rules?

Explain your game to the other groups. Then choose a game and play it as a group.

UNIT 3 Dance

You are going to read three texts about dance. First, answer the questions in the boxes.

READING 1

Have fun with dance

Read this newspaper article about dances that are both fun and good for you.

1. Do you like to dance? Why or why not?
2. What are the names of some popular dances around the world?

READING 2

Oriental dance: A dance for the whole family

Many people have the wrong idea about Oriental dance, commonly known as belly dancing. This website gives the real story.

1. What is the name of a folk dance from your country?
2. On what occasions do people in your country do folk dances?

READING 3

Enjoying ballet

Why doesn't everyone like ballet? Read what two ballet lovers write about this historic form of dance.

1. Do you like ballet? Why or why not?
2. Have you ever been to the ballet? If so, which ballet did you see? What did you think of it?

Vocabulary

Find out the meanings of the words in *italics*. Then write the name of a dance that each statement might describe.

	Name of dance
1. This dance gives people a good *aerobic workout.*	______
2. This dance involves a lot of *hip* movement.	______
3. This dance *strengthens* the stomach muscles.	______
4. This dance helps people *break the ice.*	______
5. This dance involves *physical daring.*	______
6. People do this dance on *festive occasions.*	______

Have fun with dance

1 Here goes the new exercise philosophy: If it's fun, it can be good for you. But the attraction of dance goes well beyond fitness. There's the socialization — you need not go it alone — and the satisfaction of learning something new. Ultimately, it doesn't really matter which type of dance you pick — African, tap, salsa, swing, and ballroom, or other kinds of dance — as long as you like it and as long as you keep moving.

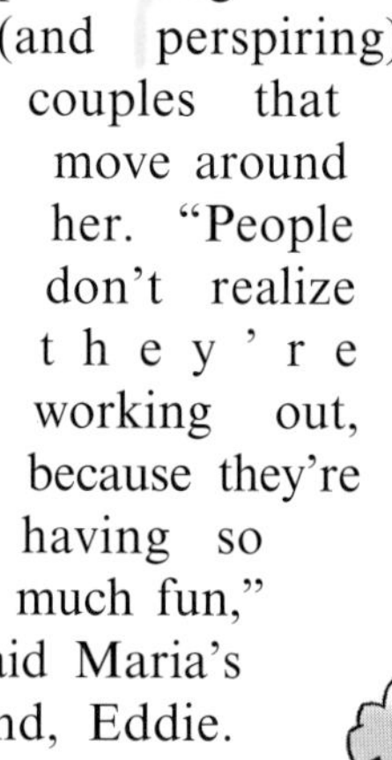
African

2 In African dance, which is accompanied by drums rather than melody, short bursts of energy alternate with long periods of movement. Different parts of the body move at different tempos, so muscles everywhere are strengthened.

3 Like other types of dance, tap can be aerobic if it's done continuously or without much of a pause. For most of us, though, tap is less of a cardiovascular workout than a lower-body workout. Tap also teaches balance and coordination and, if you do it long enough, it will strengthen your stomach muscles.

Tap

Salsa

4 Ceiling fans are set on full blast and salsa music fills the air as dance instructor Maria Torres stands in the center of the room, keeping time for the 40 hip-swiveling (and perspiring) couples that move around her. "People don't realize they're working out, because they're having so much fun," said Maria's husband, Eddie. "When you get to the intermediate levels, that's when you really start sweating," he said. "You need a change of shirt, towel, and water bottle."

5 Swing dancing can be an entertaining way to get in shape. "It's not isolating or repetitious, like riding a bike or running," says Bronwen Carson, director of a dance school. "Swing has so many different moves, you can't get bored." Bruno Bernardo, a dance instructor, adds that aside from the exercise benefits, "partner dancing is a way for people to meet others. It's a nice way to break the ice."

Swing

6 There are so many different types of ballroom dancing that almost anyone can benefit from one of them. A foxtrot or slow waltz, for instance, may be just the thing if you can't move well because of an injury or years of watching TV. A samba, on the other hand, is a good workout even for an athlete. And because ballroom dancing involves a partner, it works the arms – solo dancing usually only works the legs.

Ballroom

Adapted from *Daily News.*

READING TIP Skim the text to understand the main points. Look at things like the title, subtitles, charts, pictures, and graphs.

Before you read

Relating to the topic

Check (✔) the types of dance that you think are good forms of exercise.

_____ 1. African

_____ 2. Tap

_____ 3. Salsa

_____ 4. Swing

_____ 5. Ballroom

Reading

Skimming

Skim the text to check your answers. Then read the whole text.

After you read

Recognizing sources

A The text is from a newspaper. Check (✔) the other information you think is in the article.

_____ 1. other exercises that are good for your heart

_____ 2. other fun ways you can meet people

_____ 3. places where you can take dance classes

Guessing meaning from context

B Find the words in italics in the reading. Then complete the sentences.

ultimately (par. 1)	*full blast* (par. 4)	*waltz* (par. 6)
melody (par. 2)	*swivel* (par. 4)	*samba* (par. 6)
cardiovascular (par. 3)	*foxtrot* (par. 6)	*solo* (par. 6)

1. If you ___*swivel*___ your hips, you turn them from side to side.
2. A __________ activity is one that you do alone.
3. __________, __________, and __________ are the names of dances.
4. __________ exercise strengthens your heart and lungs.
5. A __________ is a tune that often forms part of a larger piece of music.
6. __________, you don't have to be able to dance well to stay in shape.
7. When the air conditioner is set on maximum, it is at __________.

Relating reading to personal experience

C Answer these questions.

1. Which of these dances have you tried? Which would you like to learn? Why?
2. What kind of dancing do you prefer, partner dancing or solo dancing? Why?
3. Where is the best place to go dancing where you live? Why?

Oriental dance:
A dance for the whole family

1 Although many Westerners think of belly dancing as a dance performed by a woman for a male audience, this is not the case. Oriental dance, the correct name for belly dancing, did not actually originate as a dance by women for men.

2 For centuries, the role of Oriental dance in Middle Eastern society has been that of a folk dance that people would do at joyous occasions such as weddings, the birth of a child, community festivals, and other events that bring people together to celebrate. It was a dance that men, women, and children did for fun, not a "performance" done to entertain an audience.

3 After the seventh century, people began to live in segregated households. The men lived on one side of the house, and the women lived with the children on the other side.

4 Even when there were festive occasions, the women would celebrate with other women, and the men would have a separate party with other men. Historically, the two genders did not mix. In fact, in some countries, this is still true today.

5 On special occasions, the women would meet in the afternoon, after feeding the men the big meal of the day. The women gathered to enjoy some time together in the homes of their sisters, aunts, cousins, friends, or grandmothers. At these informal get-togethers, they might take turns getting up and dancing for each other. This was one way that the mother of marriageable young men could get to know the eligible young women of the community.

6 There was generally no special dance "costume" to wear — people simply danced in their party clothes, just as we might dress up a little for our own friends' weddings. Dance was not seen as something to be "performed" by a professional — it was just something people got up and did spontaneously.

7 Today professional dancers perform at nightclubs and are often hired to entertain at weddings and other special occasions. However, for Middle Eastern people, the dance remains something that people of all ages do for fun when they get together with friends and family.

Adapted from *www.shira.net.*

Predicting

Before you read

Look at the picture on the opposite page and the words and phrases below. Find out the meanings of any words you don't know. Then check (✔) those you think you will read in the text.

____ 1. *a dance by women*
____ 2. *male audience*
____ 3. *Middle Eastern society*
____ 4. *a modern dance*
____ 5. *festive occasions*
____ 6. *costume*
____ 7. *a good form of exercise*
____ 8. *people of all ages*

Scanning

Reading

Scan the text to check your predictions. Then read the whole text.

After you read

Understanding details

A Mark the sentences true (*T*), false (*F*), or does not give the information (*?*).

_*T*_ 1. Oriental dance began in the Middle East.
____ 2. The writer is a belly dancer.
____ 3. Oriental dance is no longer common in the Middle East.
____ 4. Oriental dance began as a dance by women for women.
____ 5. Nowadays families only do Oriental dancing at weddings.
____ 6. In Middle Eastern society there are professional Oriental dancers.
____ 7. It is easier for some people to do Oriental dancing than it is for others.
____ 8. For people from the Middle East, Oriental dancing is a way to have fun.

Restating

B Compare the meaning of each pair of sentences. Write same (*S*) or different (*D*).

_*S*_ 1. After the seventh century, people began to live in segregated households.
After the seventh century, males and females lived in separate parts of the home.

____ 2. Historically, the two genders did not mix.
History shows that it's not good for men and women to mix.

____ 3. This was one way that the mother of marriageable young men could get to know the eligible young women of the community.
This was one way for a mother to meet a possible wife for her son.

Relating reading to personal experience

C Answer these questions.

1. In what ways is Oriental dance similar to folk dancing in your country? In what ways is it different?
2. What would you tell a foreign visitor who wanted to learn about folk dancing in your country?
3. What do you prefer to do at parties: dance, talk, or eat? Why?

Enjoying ballet

1 It is very odd that no one is afraid of the word "dance" and no one would object to the phrase "let's go dancing," but mention "ballet" and people start complaining. These social prejudices come from several misconceptions and from certain historic facts. Ballet is the Western theatrical dance form that developed over a period of four centuries. It has always depended upon government or royal support for its life. In more modern times, this support came from wealthy people who attend the ballet in beautiful theaters in some of the world's great cities. People have therefore come to see ballet as a cultural form, unfamiliar to anyone who does not come from a particular city or a particular class. Over time, ballet has developed its own language, one that many ordinary people do not understand. Being a ballet dancer involves seven years of very difficult training from an early age, yet anyone can dance at a social gathering, given a certain amount of effort and desire. The physical image of both male and female dancers is very stylized, and costuming is so unnatural in many cases, with its tights, slippers, and tutus. For these reasons, it is not possible for the general public to have the kind of identification with a ballet dancer that they often feel for an actor, film star, or athlete.

2 It is also strange that a visual art that speaks directly to the eye, in the same way a soccer match or an Olympic gymnastic contest does, still makes people apprehensive. Too often people stay away from ballet because they think they will not "understand" it. However, they never seem to find this problem when they watch popular ice dance championships on television. Nor are they afraid to express their opinions and sometimes disagree with the judges' decisions. People enjoy watching sports because they enjoy its physical daring. They appreciate athletes' superbly conditioned bodies working at maximum efficiency. If people only looked at dancing — any form of dancing — in the same way they appreciate sports, there would be fewer prejudices to overcome.

3 It is better to look at dancing with a completely untrained eye. If you ask questions and look for meanings, you will lose the great delight in seeing beautiful bodies, beautifully trained, performing beautiful movement. Understanding will come with experience, but your understanding will be of little value if you do not enjoy what you are watching.

Adapted from *How To Enjoy Ballet*.

Before you read

Relating to the topic

Check (✔) the statements you agree with.

____ 1. Ballet is not popular with my friends.

____ 2. I would need a few years of training to become a ballet dancer.

____ 3. Ballet is similar to sports in some ways.

Reading

Scanning

Scan the text to find out which statements the writer would probably agree with. Then read the whole text.

After you read

Recognizing point of view

A **Check (✔) the statement that best describes the writer's opinion.**

____ 1. Everyone can enjoy ballet.

____ 2. You can only enjoy ballet if you understand it.

____ 3. Only educated people can enjoy ballet.

Understanding main ideas

B **Circle the main idea of each paragraph.**

Paragraph 1
a. Some people like dancing, but not ballet.
b. People don't like ballet if they don't come from a big city.
c. People have prejudices against ballet for several reasons.

Paragraph 2
a. People appreciate sports more than they appreciate ballet.
b. People understand sports, but they don't understand ballet.
c. People will enjoy ballet more if they see it as a sport.

Paragraph 3
a. You don't have to understand ballet to enjoy it.
b. The best parts of ballet are the dancers' bodies and movements.
c. People learn to understand ballet after watching a few performances.

Guessing meaning from context

C **Find the words in *italics* in the reading. Then match each word with its meaning.**

__b__ 1. *prejudice* (par. 1) — a. deal successfully with

____ 2. *misconception* (par. 1) — b. an unreasonable dislike

____ 3. *given* (par. 1) — c. a wrong idea that people continue to believe

____ 4. *stylized* (par. 1) — d. using artistic forms for special effect

____ 5. *overcome* (par. 2) — e. if there is

Relating reading to personal experience

D **Answer these questions.**

1. Why do some people think ballet is more for females than for males?
2. If you met a professional ballet dancer, what would you ask him or her?
3. Have you ever taken ballet lessons? If so, when did you take them? If not, would you like to? Why or why not?

Vocabulary expansion

A **Look at each pair of sentences. How are the words in *italics* similar? How are they different?**

1. a. Some people *work out* by going to dance classes.
   b. A samba is a good *workout* even for an athlete.
2. a. The dance remains something that people of all ages do for fun when they *get together* with friends and family.
   b. In these informal *get-togethers*, women might take turns getting up and dancing for each other.

B **Read these definitions. Then complete each sentence with a noun that comes from these two-word verbs. (Note: Each noun is written as one word.)**

hang out: spend a lot of time in a place or with someone
let down: make someone feel disappointed
let up: become less in amount or stop
mix up: mistake (someone or something) for someone or something else
set up: establish or create (something)
show off: do something to make people admire you
warm up: exercise to prepare your body for dancing, singing, or sports

1. I stopped going to the dance class because I didn't like the school's *setup* .
2. We always did a five-minute ____________ before we started dancing.
3. Once the music started, there was no ____________; we danced nonstop until the end of the class.
4. There was a ______-______; I thought we were going to learn swing, but the teacher said he was going to teach us salsa.
5. The teacher was a real ______-______; he thought he was the world's best dancer.
6. I wanted to learn new dances, so it was a big ____________ to learn that the class was full.
7. Now I only dance at the ____________ where all my friends go to listen to music.

Dance and you

Do a class survey about dance. Ask these questions and two questions of your own.

1. Do you like to dance?
2. Do you prefer to dance or to watch others dance?
3. Do you like to watch dance perfomances?
4. Do you wish you were a better dancer?
5. Do you ______________________________?
6. Do you ______________________________?

UNIT 4 Helping others

You are going to read three texts about helping others. First, answer the questions below.

READING 1

If you see someone in trouble, don't just stand there

How do most people react when a stranger needs their help? Read a magazine study about the way people react in emergency situations.

1. What would you do if someone ahead of you suddenly collapsed on the sidewalk?
2. How do you think people react in an emergency when someone needs help?

READING 2

Random acts of kindness

Are we as kind as possible to others? What else could we do? This website offers some suggestions.

1. How do you feel when someone does something nice for you?
2. Do you think most people do kind things for their friends and relatives? What about for strangers?

READING 3

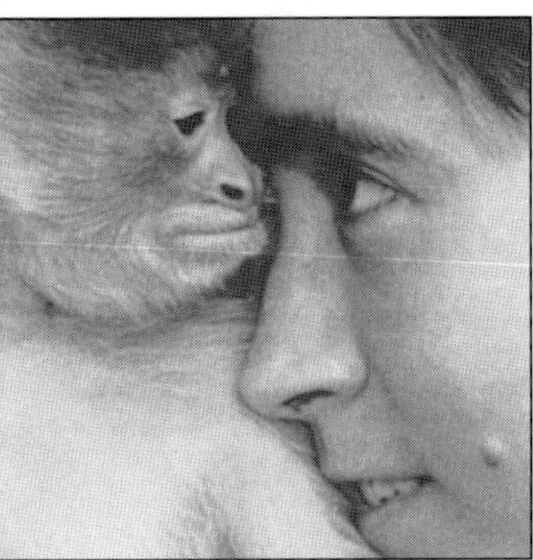

Monkey business is Henrietta's middle name

Can someone who is completely paralyzed live alone? This newspaper article explains how trained monkeys can help.

1. What kind of help does a paralyzed person need at home?
2. How can animals help disabled people?

Vocabulary

Find out the meanings of the words in *italics*. Then answer the questions.

1. Have you ever been a *bystander* at an accident?
2. What is the easiest way for a friend to *cheer* you *up*?
3. Would you *intervene* if you saw a parent hitting a child?
4. When was the last time you tried to *lift someone's spirits*?
5. Are you more *likely* to help a child or an adult?
6. Have you ever *spotted* someone in trouble? If so, were you *reluctant* to help?

If you see someone in trouble, **don't just stand there**

1 You're rushing to work and a man ahead of you collapses on the sidewalk. Do you stop to help? In a study of bystanders, it was found that some people look away or keep on walking rather than stop and get involved.

2 The question of responsibility plays an important role in preventing bystanders from doing something. In one experiment conducted by Ervin Staub, a professor of psychology at the University of Massachusetts at Amherst, an adult left groups of five-year-olds and six-year-olds in a room. The adult told some children she was leaving them in charge and they should "take care" of anything that happened. She said nothing to others. After she left, the children heard what sounded like someone in trouble in another room. The idea was to see if the children were more or less likely to help after they were told they were responsible.

3 The six-year-olds were more likely to investigate when the grown-up gave them responsibility. The five-year-olds were not. Instead, some of them even put their fingers into their ears when they heard sounds of distress. "They were in conflict," explains Staub. "They may not have felt competent or courageous enough to go into another room, but they were made responsible. So they avoided the situation."

4 According to Staub, the six-year-olds were quicker to act because they were more familiar with where to go and how to get help. Since most emergencies take place in unfamiliar settings, adults often react more like five-year-olds. They feel responsible but powerless and therefore tend to deny the crisis rather than intervene.

5 "There is an inclination to decide that no action is needed," says Staub. "The first thoughts that pop into your mind often keep you from offering help. In order to take action, you have to work against them." Common reasons that might prevent you from helping include:

- You might think someone older or with more medical knowledge should offer assistance. *Why should I be the one to help? I'm probably not the most competent person in this crowd.*
- The fear of embarrassment is powerful; no one wants to risk looking foolish in front of others. *What if he doesn't really need my help?*
- We take social cues from the people around us — but most people tend to hold back their emotions in public. *No one else looks concerned — this must not be a problem.*

6 "If you spot trouble and find yourself rationalizing inaction, force yourself to stop and evaluate the situation instead of walking on," says Staub. Then try to involve other people; you don't have to take on the entire responsibility of being helpful. "Sometimes it's just a matter of turning to the person next to you and saying, 'It looks like we should do something.' Or asking someone if an ambulance has been called and, if not, to call for one. Once you take action, most people will take their cues from you and pitch in."

Adapted from *Glamour* and *McCall's*.

Before you read

Thinking about personal experience

Check (✔) the reasons why you might *not* help others in trouble.

____ 1. You don't want to get involved.

____ 2. You don't feel qualified.

____ 3. You're not sure help is really needed.

____ 4. You're too busy to help.

____ 5. You think that someone else will help.

____ 6. The other people around you don't look concerned.

Reading

Scanning

Scan the text to find out which reasons the writer mentions. Then read the whole text.

After you read

Understanding main ideas

A Write the number of each paragraph next to its main idea.

_6_ a. This paragraph suggests ways to take action when someone needs help.

____ b. This paragraph explains why people often do not help.

____ c. This paragraph describes the steps in the experiment.

____ d. This paragraph connects the experiment to how adults react in emergencies.

____ e. This paragraph describes what happened during the experiment.

Understanding details

B Circle the answers that are true.

1. What was the plan for the experiment?
   - (a.) An adult told some of the children to take care of any problems.
   - b. An adult told all of the children to take care of any problems.
2. What happened during the experiment?
   - a. Some of the six-year-olds did something when there was a problem.
   - b. Some of the five-year-olds did something when there was a problem.
3. How should you react if you think someone might be in trouble?
   - a. Find someone older or with more medical knowledge.
   - b. Try to involve other bystanders.

Relating reading to personal experience

C Answer these questions.

1. Do you think people in your country are reluctant to help others? Why or why not?
2. What do you think is the best thing to do in each of these situations?
   - a. A group of teenagers is fighting with another group of teenagers.
   - b. Someone is screaming outside your window in the middle of the night.
   - c. Someone near you suddenly gets very ill during an important exam.
3. Have you ever needed emergency help? If so, what happened?

Random acts of kindness

1 On a cold winter day in San Francisco, a woman drives up to the Bay Bridge tollbooth. "I'm paying for myself, and for the six cars behind me," she says. Then she smiles and hands over seven commuter tickets. One after another, the next six drivers arrive at the tollbooth, money in hand, only to be told, "Some lady up ahead already paid your toll for you. Have a nice day."

2 It turned out the woman had read something a friend had taped to her refrigerator: "Practice random kindness and senseless acts of beauty." She liked the phrase so much she copied it down.

3 Judy Foreman spotted the same phrase painted on a wall a hundred miles from her home. It stayed on her mind for days, so she copied it down. "I thought it was incredibly beautiful," she said, explaining why she now puts it at the bottom of all the letters she writes.

4 Her husband Frank liked the phrase so much that he put it up on the wall for his students, one of whom was the daughter of a local newspaper columnist. The columnist put it in the newspaper, even though she wasn't sure what it really meant.

5 Two days later, she got a call from Anne Herbert. Herbert lives in Marin, California. She saw the phrase in a local restaurant, wrote it down, and thought it over for days.

6 "Here's the idea," Herbert says. "Anything you think there should be more of, do it randomly." Her own ideas include: going into depressing-looking schools to paint the classrooms; leaving hot meals on kitchen tables in the poor parts of town; slipping money into a proud old woman's purse. "Kindness can build on itself as much as violence can," says Herbert. Now the phrase is spreading, on bumper stickers, on walls, at the bottom of letters and business cards. And as it spreads, so do people's ideas about the kind things they can do for others.

7 In Portland, Oregon, a man puts a coin into a stranger's parking meter just in time. In Patterson, New Jersey, a dozen people with pails, mops, and flower seeds go to a run-down house and clean it while the elderly owners look on, shocked and smiling. A man in St. Louis, whose car has just been hit by a young woman, smiles and says, "It's a scratch. Don't worry."

8 Random acts of beauty spread. A man plants flowers along the roadway. In Seattle, another man decides that he's going to clean up the trash people have left on city streets. In Atlanta, a man removes graffiti from a park bench.

9 You can't smile without cheering yourself up a little. Likewise, you can't commit a random act of kindness without feeling as if your own troubles have been lightened. If you were one of those drivers who found your bridge toll paid, who knows what you might do for someone else later? Wave someone on in the intersection? Smile at a tired clerk? Kindness begins slowly with a single act. Try it.

READING TIP

Punctuation can help you understand the relationship between ideas. For example, the colon (:) after "Her own ideas include" shows that a list of her ideas will come next. Then a semicolon (;) separates each of her ideas.

Adapted from *www.globalideasbank.org.*

Predicting

Before you read

Check (✔) the statement that you think best explains the expression *Practice random acts of kindness.*

____ 1. Do kind things for strangers without having a good reason.

____ 2. Be nice to your friends and compliment them.

____ 3. Learn how to be kinder and more generous.

Scanning

Reading

Scan the text to check your prediction. Then read the whole text.

Recognizing purpose

After you read

A Check (✔) the writer's main purpose in writing the text.

____ 1. to tell stories about different people

____ 2. to describe true acts of kindness

____ 3. to persuade people to help others

Understanding details

B Under each picture, write a phrase that describes an act of kindness in the text.

1. *pay the toll for other drivers*

2. ____________

3. ____________

4. ____________

5. ____________

6. ____________

Relating reading to personal experience

C Answer these questions.

1. Which of the random acts of kindness described in the text might you do in the future? Which will you definitely *not* do? Why?
2. What other random acts of kindness can you think of?
3. Have you ever done something to help a stranger? If so, what?

Monkey business is Henrietta's middle name

1 When Sue Strong's Manhattan apartment grew very quiet one afternoon, she wasn't too surprised to find her monkey, Henrietta, in the bathroom amid opened jars, licking lotion off her lips.

2 Life with Henrietta is never boring. But then again, Henrietta is not just any monkey. She is one of 50 working simians in the Helping Hands program, which trains monkeys to assist quadriplegics with day-to-day tasks. "What Seeing-Eye dogs are to the blind, the monkeys are to people who can't use their hands or legs," said Jean Amaral, the program's administrator.

3 For the past 18 years, Henrietta, nicknamed Henri, has been living with Strong, who became paralyzed in a car accident. Henri helps out by turning on the TV, flicking the lights on and off, or bringing Strong a drink when she's thirsty. "Henri is a tremendous help to me," Strong said. "I can't imagine what life would be without her." Strong has a caretaker come to her home each morning and night to help her get in and out of bed, and to bathe and dress her. When the assistant leaves, Henri takes over, allowing Strong to stay alone for hours. "Without an attendant or family member around to help, if I drop the stick I hold in my mouth to lift light switches, I would be alone and in the dark," she said. "With Henri, I can spend eight hours alone and be fine."

4 Henri spends most of her day playing or napping. When Strong needs something, she shines a laser attached to her chair onto the object she wants. "Henri is trained to look for the laser light," Strong said. "When she sees the object I need, she knows what to do." Henri is trained to fetch and open jars of juice and place sandwiches in a holder. "With Henri, I usually find that I'm sharing my sandwich with her," Strong said.

5 The two have grown so close over the years that Strong considers Henri part of the family. Like all family members, Henri has her quirks. "She eats more than anyone in the house," Strong said. "Italian, Mexican, Chinese, and pizza – anything but fish. And she never gains an ounce."

6 More than helping Strong with daily tasks, Henri lifts her spirits with her irresistible charm and playful antics. "She's a diva through and through," said Strong of her 7-pound friend. While people are sometimes reluctant to approach Strong when she is out alone, they come in droves when she is with Henri.

7 Henri loves to have her hair combed. She jumps into Strong's lap and waits eagerly for her turn when Strong is getting her hair brushed. She also likes to sit in warm piles of freshly dried clothes and watch other monkeys on TV, slapping the set happily when they're on the screen. "She's got a definite opinion on everyone who walks in the house," Strong said. "Some people she loves. Others she loves to nibble at their ankles. She's even kicked some people in the behind."

Adapted from *Daily News*.

Before you read

Predicting

Check (✔) the things you think a monkey can do.

____ 1. turn on the TV

____ 2. turn the lights on and off

____ 3. bring someone a sandwich

____ 4. help someone get in and out of bed

____ 5. bathe and dress someone

____ 6. open a jar of juice

Reading

Scanning

Scan the text to check your predictions. Then read the whole text.

After you read

Recognizing similarity in meaning

A Match each word or phrase with a word or phrase that is similar in meaning.

_g_	1. *monkey* (par. 1)	a. *assist* (par. 2)
____	2. *paralyzed* (par. 3)	b. *attendant* (par.3)
____	3. *turn on* (par. 3)	c. *day-to-day* (par. 2)
____	4. *bring* (par. 3)	d. *fetch* (par. 4)
____	5. *caretaker* (par. 3)	e. *flick on* (par. 3)
____	6. *help* (par. 3)	f. *quadriplegic* (par. 2)
____	7. *daily* (par. 6)	g. *simian* (par. 2)

Understanding details

B Check (✔) the information that is mentioned in the text.

_✔_ 1. things Henrietta does for Strong

____ 2. Henrietta's age

____ 3. the amount of time it took to train Henrietta

____ 4. the name of the program that trained Henrietta

____ 5. the amount of time Henrietta has been with Strong

____ 6. whether Henrietta goes with Strong when she leaves her apartment

____ 7. Strong's feelings about Henrietta

____ 8. the kinds of problems Henrietta can cause

Relating reading to personal experience

C Answer these questions.

1. Do you think a person would be a better caregiver than Henrietta? Why or why not?
2. Do you think it is fair or unfair to train animals to help people? Why?
3. Would you like to have a monkey in your home? Why or why not?

Vocabulary expansion

A **Find the phrasal verbs below in this unit's readings. Then write the letter of the correct definition next to each phrasal verb. (Be careful! There are two extra definitions.)**

_g_ 1. *keep from* (reading 1, par. 5)
____ 2. *hold back* (reading 1, par. 5)
____ 3. *take on* (reading 1, par. 6)
____ 4. *pitch in* (reading 1, par. 6)
____ 5. *hand over* (reading 2, par. 1)
____ 6. *look on* (reading 2, par. 7)
____ 7. *take over* (reading 3, par. 3)

a. accept responsibility for something
b. take and keep something in your hand
c. do a job someone else was doing
d. give (something) to someone else
e. stop yourself from showing feelings
f. move (something) from one place to another
g. prevent (someone) from doing (something)
h. watch something without being involved in it
i. help with something that needs to be done

B **Complete each sentence with a phrasal verb from exercise A.**

1. We need all of you to ____________ . Please help.
2. Don't let fear ____________ you ____________ helping.
3. What's ____________ing you ____________ ? Help when you see a person in need before it's too late!
4. Don't just ____________ when somebody's in trouble. You can help with your hands, not with your eyes.
5. You don't need to ____________ your money. Just give us your heart and help a stranger in need.
6. We know you're a busy person. But a few minutes is all you need to help until the police come and ____________ .

Helping others and you

Work in small groups. Make a list of ways that you could help others. Think about places or organizations where you could donate money or volunteer time. Decide which activities your group would do to help others. If you give money, how much can the group raise? How will the money be earned and collected? Compare your group's decision with those of the other groups.

UNIT 5 Movies

You are going to read three texts about movies. First, answer the questions in the boxes.

READING 1

Stunt school

Do you seek danger and excitement? This newspaper article describes what it takes to be a movie stunt performer and why people choose this unusual profession.

1. What kinds of things do movie stunt performers do?
2. What qualities does a person need to be a stunt performer?

READING 2

Movie extras

Read about the non-speaking "extras" who play an important part of every movie.

1. What are some of the things that movie extras do?
2. What do you think are some advantages and disadvantages of being an extra?

READING 3

The storyteller

In this magazine article, find out what director Steven Spielberg enjoys about filmmaking.

1. Which movie director(s) do you like?
2. What movies has Steven Spielberg directed? Which of these have you seen?

Vocabulary

Find out the meanings of the words in *italics*. Then answer the questions.

1. What is the last *flick* you saw in a theater?
2. Who are the *big names* in the movies these days?
3. Have you ever been to a *film set*?
4. What movie is a *hit* in your town these days?
5. What *parts* has your favorite actor or actress played?
6. Do you like *sci-fi* movies?
7. Would you see the *sequel* of a movie you like?

Stunt school

1 Think you've had a rough day? Try this: First, you get thrown out of a car onto the expressway. Next, you fall out of a tree. Then you tumble down the stairs headfirst. To top it all off, you get set on fire . . . and it isn't even noon yet!

2 For graduates of a Toronto stunt school, this is all in a morning's work. Since opening its doors, Stunt Productions Canada has trained hundreds of would-be stunt performers. They come from all walks of life – lawyers, firefighters, retail workers, hockey players, factory workers, and almost anyone else you can think of.

3 The glory, excitement, and big pay of movie stunt work can be a powerful draw. But most people who take the Stunt Productions courses – $1,000 for the introductory course, plus another $720 for the advanced – don't intend to make a full-time career in the movies.

4 A qualified stunt performer working on a unionized Canadian film set earns a minimum of $342 a day, and top stunt performers can earn $150,000 a year or more. Big names in the business can earn $500,000 as year doing stunts and consultation work for major films. But most stunt school students will never earn more than the cost of their tuition – they're not looking for a movie career, just something that's different from their everyday lives.

5 And they get it – drops, fights, crashes, burns, drags behind cars – all are part of the school's 16-week introductory course. Those who want more can take the 12-week advanced course.

6 Almost every student who has enrolled in the school since it opened has been male, and few are over 30. In the stunt business, 40 is considered ancient.

7 So why do people want to be stunt performers? "I do it because it's fun!" says Craig Samuel, who's used his stunt school diploma to get a few movie parts. "Stunt men tend to be people searching for the edge. The trick is whether you go over it or not."

8 "I don't usually tell people I'm a stunt man," he says. "They always say, 'Oh, you're a daredevil!' But you're not a daredevil. The key to stunt work is being careful so you don't get hurt . . . I don't want to die."

9 Despite the precautions the pros take, there is danger. "Of course there's danger," says school owner Parr. "Stunt men get killed sometimes. It happens." Dar Robinson, the famous stunt man who jumped twice from the CN Tower for movies, was killed riding a motorcycle during a routine, low-risk film sequence.

10 "It was pretty ironic," Parr says. "When you consider all the dangerous things he'd done."

11 "If you're not prepared to get banged around a little bit, you shouldn't be in it," says Samuel. "Some mornings you can't get your head off the pillow."

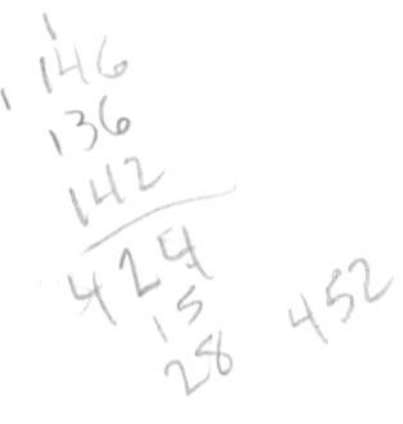

Adapted from *The Toronto Star*.

Relating to the topic

Before you read

Check (✔) the statements you think are true.

____ 1. Stunt performers come from all walks of life — lawyers, firefighters, retail workers, and so on.

____ 2. Stunt performers are usually people who can't find other work.

____ 3. Most stunt performers earn a lot of money.

____ 4. People go to stunt school to have a career in the movies.

____ 5. Stunt work looks dangerous, but it really isn't.

Scanning

Reading

Scan the text to check your answers. Then read the whole text.

After you read

Guessing meaning from context

A Find the words in *italics* in the reading. Circle the meaning of each word.

1. *Would-be* stunt performers are **hopeful** / **afraid** of finding stunt work. (par. 2)
2. If something is *a draw*, it is **a picture** / **an attraction**. (par. 3)
3. If people are searching for *the edge*, they're looking for **more excitement** / **the correct way to do something**. (par. 7)
4. A *daredevil* likes doing **strange** / **dangerous** things. (par. 8)
5. When you take *precautions* you try to **prepare someone to do a good job** / **prevent something bad from happening**. (par. 9)
6. If something is *low-risk*, there is little **cost** / **danger**. (par. 9)

Understanding details

B Answer the questions. Write (?) if the text does not give the information.

1. What are some of the things students practice in stunt school?
   Students practice being dropped, fighting, crashing, and being dragged behind cars.
2. How many Stunt Productions Canada graduates work as stunt performers?
   ____
3. How much do courses cost, and how long do they last?
   ____
4. Why do most stunt school students attend the school?
   ____
5. What movies have the school's graduates worked in?
   ____
6. What was ironic about the way Dar Robinson died?
   ____

Relating reading to personal experience

C Answer these questions.

1. Would you be interested in attending stunt school? Why or why not?
2. Which would you rather do — act in a movie or perform the stunts? Why?
3. Have you seen a movie that had good stunts? If so, what stunts were used?

Movie extras

1 Would you mind lying in a coffin? Would you shave your head? Are you willing to take out your false teeth?

2 These are just a few of the questions Anne Marie Stewart and her staff sometimes ask the "talent" who serve as non-speaking "extras" in feature films, television series, and made-for-TV movies produced in Toronto. At short notice, her agency has filled requests for a Pamela Lee Anderson lookalike, someone who could pass for a sumo wrestler, and a person missing two fingers on one hand. The list goes on and on.

3 Of course, the majority of extra calls are for more ordinary people, and Stewart has a list of about 650 registered extras. Crowd scenes, which are common, call for everyday people of all ages, ethnic backgrounds, and sizes.

4 Over at Movie People, last-minute requests are not unusual. "We got a request once for an entire brass band. They wanted it within the hour," said manager Yvonne McCartney. Another time, the company got a last-minute request for a newborn baby. "We found a baby that was three weeks premature," said Jonathan Aiken, an owner of the company.

5 Then there was the panicky call from a casting director whose "star" got doggone stubborn one day and decided to just lie down and not work. It was a dilemma of Dalmatian dimensions. The director needed a replacement dog, fast. "We got them two Dalmatians in one hour," said Aiken. "It was a matter of good connections and fast phone work." The eight phone lines needed to make 350 to 400 calls a day are one of Movie People's major expenses.

6 Phone lines are the only way to stay in touch with casting directors and extras; but the latter are a group not necessarily interested in a long-term relationship. Most extra jobs pay only \$7 an hour (with a six-hour minimum), while most agencies charge an annual \$75 registration fee and get a 10 to 15 per cent commission on extras' earnings. It's no wonder that the turnover rate is fairly high.

7 Some people who are between jobs do extra work as a temporary measure, said McCartney. But professionals, such as lawyers, also do the work because it's interesting. Others with flexible jobs have a desire to do something different. Some homemakers want to get out of the house and onto a movie set. Money's not the motivating factor.

8 "One of the first things I say to people who walk in and ask about being an extra is, 'you have to be available,'" said Karen Clifton of Karen Clifton Agency, Inc. "The next thing I say is, 'you can't make a living at this.' "

9 Clifton uses two computers for the business "but the best computer is my head," she said. "You have to have a certain eye in this work. You have to know instinctively who's best." Occasionally, the "best" person for an extra role – especially if it's a "bum" – is her husband Alan, who already has a collection of clothes for the part. "He's the only bum you'll ever see carrying a cell phone," she laughed.

READING TIP Quotation marks (" ") around a word can show a special meaning that is a little different from its meaning in the dictionary. For example, *talent* in this text is not "a natural ability to do something well," but "film extras."

Adapted from *The Toronto Star*.

Before you read

Predicting

Look at the title and the picture on the opposite page. Then check (✔) the information you think you will read about in the text.

____ 1. the names of agencies that find extras for movies

____ 2. the kinds of extras needed for movies

____ 3. the names of movies that extras have worked on

____ 4. the pay rates for extras

____ 5. the ways that some extras become movie stars

____ 6. the reasons why people want to work as extras

Reading

Scanning

Scan the text to check your predictions. Then read the whole text.

After you read

Recognizing sources

A **Where does the text probably come from? Check (✔) the correct answer.**

____ 1. an encyclopedia

____ 2. an article in a newspaper

____ 3. a history of the movie industry

____ 4. the classified ads in a newspaper

Understanding details

B **Circle the answer that is *not* true.**

1. What is true about movie extras?
   a. They usually have to have special talents.
   b. They have to be ready to work right away.
   c. They can't
2. Why do peo[...]
   a. They have [...] yet.
   b. They want
   c. They want
3. How much [...] agency?
   a. $75 every
   b. 10 to 15 [...]
   c. $75 every [...] jobs
4. What do pe[...]ul movie-extra agency?
   a. They have to be able to work fast.
   b. They have to have dedicated people working for them.
   c. They have to make lots of phone calls.

Relating reading to personal experience

C **Answer these questions.**

1. What do you think would be interesting about being a movie extra?
2. Which movies do you wish you could have been an extra in?
3. If you got a job as an extra, what parts would you like to play?

The storyteller

1 Steven Spielberg has always had one goal: to tell as many great stories to as many people as will listen. And that's what he has always been about. The son of a computer scientist and a pianist, Spielberg spent his early childhood in New Jersey and, later, Arizona. From the very beginning, his fertile imagination filled his young mind with images that would later inspire his filmmaking.

2 Even decades later, Spielberg says he has vivid memories of his earliest years, which are the origins of some of his biggest hits. He believes that *E.T.* is the result of the difficult years leading up to his parent's 1966 divorce, saying, "It is really about a young boy who was in search of some stability in his life." *Close Encounters of the Third Kind* was inspired by early morning meteor-gazing with his father, a sci-fi fanatic, when he was four years old. "He was scared of just about everything," recalls his mother, Leah Adler. "When trees brushed against the house, he would head into my bed. And that's just the kind of scary stuff he would put in films like *Poltergeist*." To this day, Spielberg's wife, actress Kate Capshaw, says her husband remains terrified of airplane and elevator rides and closed-in places.

3 After the family moved to California, Spielberg's grades in high school got worse and worse. He barely graduated and was rejected from both UCLA and USC film schools. Settling for California State University at Long Beach because it was close to Hollywood, he got a C in his television production course. He dropped out during his senior year.

4 It was all very sobering, especially since Spielberg had long since made up his mind to become a director. The homemade movies he started making as a young boy gave Spielberg a powerful escape from his fears. He was 11 when he first got his hands on his dad's movie camera and began shooting short flicks about flying saucers and World War II battles.

5 Spielberg's talent for scary storytelling enabled him to torture his three younger sisters and made it easier for him to make friendships. On Boy Scout camping trips, when night fell, Spielberg became the center of attention. "Stevie would start telling his ghost stories," says Richard Y. Hoffman, Jr., leader of Troop 294, "and everyone would suddenly get quiet so that they could all hear it."

6 Now, many years later, Spielberg is still telling stories with as much passion as the kid in the tent. Ask him where he gets his ideas, and Spielberg shrugs. "The process for me is mostly intuitive," he says. "There are films that I feel that I need to make, for a variety of reasons, for personal reasons, for reasons that I want to have fun, that the subject matter is cool, that I think my kids will like it. And sometimes I just think that it will make a lot of money, like the sequel to *Jurassic Park*."

Adapted from *Business Week*.

Before you read

Predicting

Look at the title on the opposite page and the words and phrases below. Find out the meanings of any words you don't know. Then check (✔) those you think you will read in the text.

____	1. *stories*	____	6. *movie stars*
____	2. *books*	____	7. *homemade movies*
____	3. *imagination*	____	8. *have fun*
____	4. *filmmaking*	____	9. *handsome*
____	5. *terrified*	____	10. *a lot of money*

Reading

Scanning

Scan the text to check your predictions. Then read the whole text.

After you read

Guessing meaning from context

A **Find the words in *italics* in the reading. Then match each word with its meaning. (Be careful! There is one extra answer.)**

_b_	1. *fertile* (par. 1)	a. very clear
____	2. *vivid* (par. 2)	b. creative
____	3. *stability* (par. 2)	c. permanence
____	4. *fanatic* (par. 2)	d. causing a person to think seriously
____	5. *sobering* (par. 4)	e. complain about things that happened long ago
		f. someone who is very enthusiastic about something

Making inferences

B **Check (✔) the statements you think Spielberg would say.**

_✓_ 1. I've always been good at telling stories.

____ 2. My parents weren't happy together. However, that didn't bother me because I had a great imagination.

____ 3. If students don't do well in school, they won't succeed.

____ 4. I have never understood why people get scared when they see my movies.

____ 5. I wanted to work in the movies because I didn't finish college.

____ 6. Making movies can be fun.

____ 7. Money isn't important to me.

Relating reading to personal experience

C **Answer these questions.**

1. Who is the most successful movie director in your country?
2. Who is more important for a movie's success, the director or the actors? Why?
3. Does a good movie need to have a good story? Which movies have good stories?

Vocabulary expansion

A **Complete the diagrams with the words from the box. Then add your own word to each diagram.**

acting	animation	characters	dramas	plot	special effects
actors	cameraperson	comedies	extras	sci-fi	stunts
actresses	cast	director	horror	script	thrillers

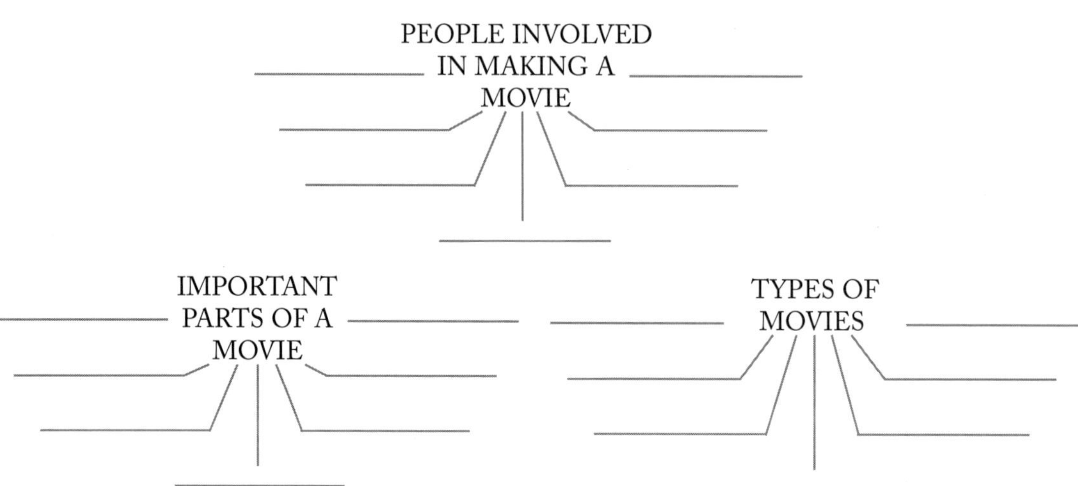

B **Use the words from exercise A to answer the questions. Then compare your answers with another student.**

1. What person or people do you think are most important in making a movie?
2. What do you think are the two most important parts of a movie?
3. What are your two favorite types of movies?

Movies and you

Work in small groups. Make a list of some movies people in the group have seen recently. Next, discuss the movies and assign each a rating from one star (A waste of time and money) to four stars (Excellent). Finally, choose one movie and write your own review of it. Should you recommend that others go see it? Why or why not? Remember to give the movie a rating and be specific when explaining your decision.

**** Excellent. You'll love it.
*** Very good. You'll enjoy it, but it's not perfect.
** OK.
* A waste of time and money.

UNIT 6 Families

You are going to read three texts about families. First, answer the questions in the boxes.

READING 1

Living with mother

This newspaper article reports on a different type of marriage custom in a region of southwest China.

1. How large is your family? Do you live with or near all of your relatives?
2. In your culture, does property pass down through the mother or the father?

READING 2

Father's Day

In this excerpt from a memoir, the writer describes the special relationship he had with his aunt.

1. What are some things boys usually learn from their fathers?
2. Is there a special day to honor fathers in your country? If so,what happens on that day?

READING 3

The incredible shrinking family

Read from a book that explains how families in the United States are changing.

1. Who has more brothers and sisters, you or your parents?
2. Do you think a wife should contribute to a household's income? Why or why not?

Vocabulary

Find out the meanings of the words in *italics*. Then check (✔) the statements you agree with.

____ 1. *Raising* children is primarily a woman's responsibility.

____ 2. Married couples who are *childless* cannot be happy.

____ 3. Children who *grow up* in two-parent families are happier than children in single-parent families.

____ 4. Girls and boys should be *brought up* differently.

____ 5. Fathers should be more involved in their children's *upbringing*.

____ 6. Life is easier for a family when a man is the *head of the household*.

Living with mother

In southwest China, the Mosuo people have found the secret of a happy family life: No one ever leaves their mother's home. But your partner is only a walk away.

1 Tseta Dashi is twenty-nine and the proud father of a five-month old daughter. He does not see his baby much because both mother and daughter live in another village, about twelve miles away.

2 Dashi prefers to continue living with his mother, along with his mother's brother, his own two brothers, his younger sister, Pizuchuma, and her two daughters. And where is Dashi's father? He has always lived with his own mother and rarely visits these days. Dashi's older brother has two children, but they live with their mother. The father of Pizuchuma's children still lives with his mother.

3 It all sounds very complicated, but it's not. In Luoshui village, the Tseta family is normal. This area of China is home to the Mosuo people. For the Mosuo, there is no notion of formal marriage and no marriage ceremony. Instead, the Mosuo have what are called "walking marriages."

4 In Mosuo society, the adult children, men and women, live in their mother's home even after they have found a partner; "walking marriages" make for a lot of coming and going in the evenings. Most nights, Dashi's older brother walks across the village to visit his partner and children; he returns home for breakfast. Pizuchuma's partner, who also lives in the same village, arrives at the Tseta house in the evening and leaves in the morning. Dashi, with twelve miles to travel, has more of a "bicycle marriage" and only gets to see his partner and new baby about twice a month.

5 "Walking marriages" have many effects on family life. For example, Pizuchuma's youngest daughter is the same age as Dashi's. Dashi is clear about his feelings. "I am closer to my nieces than to my daughter, because I must always consider their upbringing and their education." It is Dashi and his brothers who are financially responsible for Pizuchuma's children, not their father. And when Dashi was growing up, the most important man in his life was not his father, but his mother's brother. Similarly, Dashi's baby girl will be brought up by her uncles.

6 Children take their mother's family name, and property passes down through the mother. The head of the household is always the oldest woman – the aju. "In Mosuo society the uncle is more powerful than the father," says the Luoshui village headman. "Inside the home, the mother is more powerful than the uncle."

7 "Walking marriages" can start from the age of seventeen or eighteen. Couples decide how often they want to see each other. "Maybe not every day," says Guambu Ager, a Mosuo scholar. When the first child is born, the father's family bring presents to the mother's family aju in a "declaration of the relationship."

8 Mosuo "divorce" is very simple. Couples stop the walking marriage if they stop getting along. It is quite easy to split up, explains Ager. "As men and women do not set up house together, all the household is from the mother's family, so there are no quarrels. It is very harmonious."

Adapted from *The Independent.*

Before you read

Predicting

Look at the title and introduction on the opposite page. Then check (✔) the information you think you will read about in the text.

_____ 1. After marriage, husbands do not live with their wives or children.

_____ 2. After marriage, wives live with their husband's family.

_____ 3. There is no divorce.

_____ 4. There is no marriage ceremony.

_____ 5. Children take their father's family name.

_____ 6. The head of the household is always the oldest woman.

Reading

Scanning

Scan the text to check your predictions. Then read the whole text.

After you read

Summarizing

A Check (✔) the best summary of the text.

_____ 1. The Mosuo get married when they are 17 or 18.

_____ 2. The article is about Tseta Dashi and his family.

_____ 3. This article is about the Mosuo, who live in southwest China.

_____ 4. The Mosuo live with their mothers after they marry.

Understanding details

B Write the numbers of the family members in the correct houses.

1. Tseta Dashi
2. Tseta Dashi's wife
3. Tseta Dashi's daughter
4. Tseta Dashi's mother
5. Tseta Dashi's father
6. Tseta Dashi's brothers
7. Tseta Dashi's older brother's children
8. Tseta Dashi's older brother's wife
9. Pizuchuma, Tseta Dashi's sister
10. Pizuchuma's husband
11. Pizuchuma's two daughters
12. Tseta Dashi's father's mother
13. Tseta Dashi's mother's brother
14. Pizuchuma's mother-in-law

House A	House B	House C	House D	House E
1 ___ ___ ___ ___ ___	___ ___	___ ___	___ ___	___ ___

Relating reading to personal experience

C Answer these questions.

1. What are the advantages of Mosuo marriage customs? The disadvantages?
2. Do you think the Mosuo would like marriage customs in your society? Why or why not?
3. Does it matter whether fathers or uncles bring up children? Why or why not?

Father's Day

Each June, I honor my Aunt Marion, who taught me the things my father couldn't.

1 My father was 27 when he died. Over the years, the image I had of him was formed from all the stories I had heard. I was a few months old when he died, and a single photograph of me in his arms is the only hard evidence I have that we ever met.

2 After my father's death, my mother moved back to Louisville, Kentucky, where she had grown up. We lived in a small house with her older sister, Marion, and their mother. This was a time when being a single parent was still considered unusual.

3 When I was small, there was a children's book called *The Happy Family*, and it was a real piece of work. Dad worked all day long at the office, Mom baked in the kitchen, and brother and sister always had friends sleeping over. The image of the family in this book was typical of the time. It looked nothing like my family, but luckily that wasn't the way I heard it. The way my Aunt Marion read it to me, the story was really funny.

4 Compassionate and generous, opinionated yet open-minded, my aunt was the one who played baseball with me in the early summer evenings, who took me horseback riding, and who sat by my bed when I was ill. She helped me find my first job and arranged for her male friends at work to take me to the father-son dinners that marked the end of every sports season. When the time came, she convinced the elderly man next door to teach me how to shave. When I was 15, she gave me lessons on how to drive. Believing that anything unusual was probably good for me, she offered to get a loan so that I could go to Africa to work as a volunteer. She even paid for my first typewriter.

5 As a young girl, Aunt Marion always planned to have a large number of children of her own, but she never got married. This meant that she was free to spend all her time taking care of me. Many people say we're very much alike: stubborn, determined, softhearted, and opinionated. We argued often. She always expected me to do my best. She never failed to assure me that I could do anything with my life that I wanted, if I only tried hard enough.

6 For more than sixty years, Aunt Marion was never without a job of some kind. In a fairer world, she would have been the boss. But being Aunt Marion, she didn't and still doesn't give herself much credit. Unless forced to come up to the front, she stands in the back in family photos and doesn't think that her efforts have made much difference. So every June for the past 40 years, in growing appreciation of my Aunt Marion, I've sent her a Father's Day card.

Adapted from *Paper Trail.*

Before you read

Predicting

Look at the title and introduction on the opposite page. Then answer these questions.

1. What do you think the writer and his Aunt Marion did together?
2. Why do you think the writer's father couldn't teach him?
3. Why do you think the writer chose the title "Father's Day"?

Reading

Scanning

Scan the text to check your predictions. Then read the whole text.

After you read

Understanding details

A **Mark each sentence true (*T*) or false (*F*). Then correct the false sentences.**

F 1. The writer's ~~mother~~ *father* died when he was very young.

____ 2. The writer lived in Louisville, Kentucky, before his father's death.

____ 3. The writer had an unhappy childhood.

____ 4. Aunt Marion did many of the things a father usually does.

____ 5. Aunt Marion never wanted to get married and have children.

____ 6. The writer and his aunt have similar personalities.

____ 7. Aunt Marion lived with the writer when he was growing up.

____ 8. The writer began to appreciate Aunt Marion more as an adult.

Summarizing

B **Write complete sentences about the writer's family life.**

1. This is why the writer's family wasn't anything like the family in *The Happy Family*:
His father was dead, his mother didn't bake in the kitchen all day, and he had no brothers or sisters.

2. These are things Aunt Marion did for the writer when he was young:

3. These are things Aunt Marion did for the writer when he was older:

4. These are things Aunt Marion had to ask men to do because she couldn't:

Relating reading to personal experience

C **Answer these questions.**

1. Who in your family are you closest to? What makes this person special?
2. What is a special memory you have from your childhood?
3. Who in your family are you most like? How are you similar?

The incredible shrinking family

1 People's attitudes about the role of women in marriage and work have changed with the shifting American economy. In the late 1970s, most Americans felt that wives *shouldn't* contribute to the income of a household. By the late eighties, a small majority (51.7 percent) still continued to hold this view. By the early nineties, however, a majority agreed that wives *should* contribute to the income of a household. By the late nineties, two-thirds of the American population felt this way. Similarly, in the mid-1970s, almost two-thirds of the people felt it was "Much better for everyone involved if the man is the achiever outside the home and the woman takes care of the home and family." But by the end of the nineties, two-thirds disagreed with this view.

2 So it's not surprising that, as the economy has changed, the birthrate among married women has steadily dropped: from ninety-eight births per 1,000 married women twenty years ago to eighty in the late 1990s. In all likelihood, as the new economy becomes stronger, that rate will continue to drop. In fact, it's no longer unusual for a woman to decide not to have children altogether. In the mid-1970s, only about ten percent of middle-aged women had never had a child. Among them were teachers, nuns, or nurses, who had dedicated their lives to their work. Their decision to be childless was respected but also set them apart, into their own childless subculture. Now, a decision not to have children isn't so odd. Nineteen percent of women between the ages of forty and forty-five have never had a child. Some of them are happily married. They're just pursuing interests other than raising children.

3 Even women who plan to have children are delaying. Births to very young women have dropped dramatically. By the year 2000, it reached the lowest rate in the United States since 1906, when the government began keeping records on birthrates. The same pattern holds true for all racial and ethnic groups. Birthrates for women in their twenties, meanwhile, haven't changed. The only increase in birthrates has been among women in their thirties. In the state of Massachusetts, more babies are now born to women over thirty than under thirty.

4 Whether women are heading into paid work in order to improve the family income or to pursue greater opportunities, families are shrinking in response. As a result of women not being able to afford to have children, not being able to give them the time and energy that they require, or both, women are having fewer children, or no children at all.

READING TIP

Paragraphs in English have one main idea, which is often stated in the first sentence. The following sentences usually provide specific examples to support this statement. In this text, for example, the first sentence of paragraph 3 tells you that the paragraph will be about women who delay having children. The remaining sentences give details to support this fact.

Adapted from *The Future of Success*.

Using previous knowledge

Before you read

Look at the statements about families in the United States. Then circle the information you think is correct.

1. In the late 1970s, **more / fewer** than 50 percent of Americans thought women shouldn't contribute to the household income.
2. At the end of the 1990s, **one-third / two-thirds** of Americans thought women should contribute to the household income.
3. The number of births per 1,000 married women has **dropped / increased.**
4. **More / Fewer** women than before do not want to have any children.
5. Women over 30 are having **more / fewer** children than before.

Scanning

Reading

Scan the text to check your answers. Then read the whole text.

After you read

Guessing meaning from context

A Find the words in *italics* in the reading. Circle the meaning of each word.

1. *shrinking* (title and par. 4)
   (a.) getting smaller
   b. getting bigger
   c. staying the same
2. *hold this view* (par. 1)
   a. look at a picture
   b have the opinion
   c. keep something in the hand
3. *pursuing interests* (par. 2)
   a. participating in activities
   b. making money
   c. getting jobs
4. *delaying* (par. 3)
   a. thinking about something
   b. changing one's mind
   c. waiting

Understanding main ideas

B Match each paragraph with its main idea.

b 1. Paragraph 1
____ 2. Paragraph 2
____ 3. Paragraph 3
____ 4. Paragraph 4

a. Women are having fewer children than before or no children at all.
b. People's ideas about the role of women have changed.
c. Women are waiting longer to have children.
d. Because women are working more outside the home, families are getting smaller.

Relating reading to personal experience

C Answer these questions.

1. Which information in the text is also true about your country? Which information is different?
2. Do you hope to have children? Why or why not? If so, how many?
3. How has the role of women in your country changed in the past 30 years? Do you think this change has been positive or negative?

Vocabulary expansion

A **Compound adjectives can be written with a hyphen (-), as in *open-minded*, or as one word, as in *softhearted*. Complete each sentence with a compound adjective.**

1. A person with an open mind is _open-minded_.
2. A person with a soft heart is _softhearted_.
3. A person with a hard heart is ______________.
4. A person with a narrow mind is ______-______.
5. A person with a big head is ______________.
6. A person with a clear head is ______________.
7. A person with a warm heart is ______________.
8. A person with a good nature is ______-______.
9. A person with a hot head is ______________.

B **Write the correct compound adjective from exercise A next to its meaning.**

A person who is . . .

1. _softhearted_ is kind, gentle, and thinks about what other people need.
2. ______________ is not kind or understanding of the problems other people have.
3. ______________ is kind and affectionate.
4. ______________ is friendly, helpful, and doesn't get angry easily.
5. ______________ gets angry too quickly and reacts without thinking.
6. ______________ listens to other people and considers new ideas, suggestions, and opinions.
7. ______________ is able to think clearly.
8. ______________ thinks he or she is better than other people.
9. ______________ does not accept other ideas and opinions.

Families and you

Work in pairs. Talk about people in your extended families. Discuss these questions.

1. Who has a good sense of humor?
2. Who has an interesting job?
3. Who has a good personality?
4. Who has a strong interest in something?

UNIT 7 Men & women

You are going to read three texts about men and women. First, answer the questions in the boxes.

READING 1

The knight in shining armor

Do you enjoy fairy tales? This story from a popular novel teaches an important lesson about men and women.

1. What was your favorite fairy tale when you were a child?
2. What are some things that typically happen to females in fairy tales? What about males?

READING 2

Men, women, and sports

Read this magazine article to learn how men and women react differently to sports programs on TV.

1. Do you ever watch sports on TV? If so, what kinds of sports?
2. What do you like or dislike about watching sports on TV?

READING 3

Barefoot in the Park

This excerpt from a play shows how sometimes even a small incident can become a big problem in a relationship.

1. How long should people know each other before they get married?
2. If a couple has a problem, should they talk about it? Why or why not?

Vocabulary

Find out the meanings of the words in *italics*. Then check (✔) the answers you think are true.

	Men	Women
1. Who *cries out for help* more often?		
2. Who *gets depressed* more often?		
3. Who is more interested in *companionship*?		
4. Who *puts off household chores* more often.		
5. Who tries harder to *limit their intake* of junk food?		
6. Who *controls their emotions* more often?		
7. Who uses more *common sense*?		

The knight in shining armor

1 A knight in shining armor was traveling through the countryside. Suddenly, he heard a woman crying out. He raced to the castle, where the princess was trapped by a dragon. The noble knight pulled out his sword and killed the dragon. As a result, he was received lovingly by the princess.

2 As the gates opened, he was welcomed and celebrated by the family of the princess and the townspeople. He was acknowledged as a hero. He and the princess fell in love.

3 A month later, the noble knight went off on another trip. On his way back, he heard his beloved princess crying out for help. Another dragon was attacking the castle. When the knight arrived, he pulled out his sword to slay the dragon.

4 Before he swung, the princess cried out from the tower, "Don't use your sword, use this noose. It will work better."

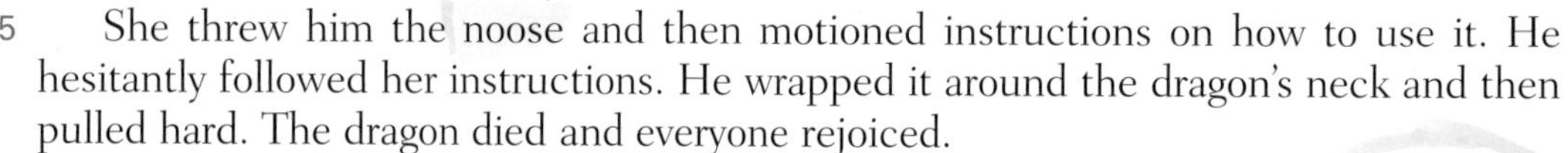

5 She threw him the noose and then motioned instructions on how to use it. He hesitantly followed her instructions. He wrapped it around the dragon's neck and then pulled hard. The dragon died and everyone rejoiced.

6 At the celebration dinner, the knight felt he hadn't really done anything. Somehow, because he had used her noose and not his sword, he didn't feel worthy of the town's admiration. After the event, he was depressed and forgot to shine his armor.

7 A month later he went on another trip. As he left with his sword, the princess reminded him to be careful and to take the noose. On his way home, he saw yet another dragon attacking the castle. This time he rushed forward with his sword but hesitated, thinking that maybe he should use the noose. In confusion, he looked up and saw his princess waving from the castle window.

8 "Use the poison," she yelled. "The noose doesn't work."

9 She threw him the poison, which he poured into the dragon's mouth, and the dragon died. Everyone rejoiced and celebrated, but the knight felt ashamed.

10 A month later, he went on another trip. As he left with his sword, the princess reminded him to be careful, and to bring the noose and the poison. He was annoyed by her suggestions but brought them just in case.

11 This time on his journey he heard another woman in distress. As he rushed to her call, his depression was lifted and he felt confident and alive. But as he drew his sword to slay the dragon, he hesitated again. He wondered whether he should use the sword, the noose, or the poison. What would the princess say?

12 For a moment he was confused. But then he remembered how he had felt before he knew the princess, when he carried only a sword. He threw away the noose and poison and charged the dragon with his sword. He slew the dragon and the townspeople rejoiced.

13 The knight in shining armor never returned to his princess. He stayed in this new village and lived happily ever after. He eventually married, but only after making sure his new partner knew nothing about nooses and poisons.

READING TIP

Always pay attention to pronouns — like *her*, *it*, and *them*. They are important for understanding the meaning of the text. For example, *he* in the first line refers to "a knight in shining armor." Pronouns also keep the names from being repeated again and again.

Adapted from *Men are from Mars, Women are from Venus.*

Before you read

Predicting

You are going to read a fairy tale involving a knight, a princess, and a dragon. Write three things you think will happen in the story.

1. ______________________________

2. ______________________________

3. ______________________________

Reading

Scanning

Scan the text to check your predictions. Then read the whole text.

After you read

Guessing meaning from context

A Find the words in *italics* in the reading. Circle the meaning of each word.

1. When a man *slays* something, he **kills** / **saves** it. (par. 3)
2. When a hero is *acknowledged*, he is **known and accepted** / **given a lot of money.** (par. 2)
3. Someone who *is beloved* **loves** / **is loved by** one or more people. (par. 3)
4. When you *motion* to someone, you **stay very still** / **move your hands or head.** (par. 5)
5. If you are *worthy*, you **deserve admiration** / **are worth a lot of money.** (par. 6)
6. If you *hesitate*, you **change your mind** / **stop for a moment.** (par. 7)
7. When you are *in distress*, you are **ill** / **in danger.** (par. 11)

Understanding a sequence of events

B Number the sentences from 1 (first event) to 7 (last event).

____ a. The knight got married.

__1__ b. The knight killed a dragon with a sword.

____ c. The knight killed a dragon with a sword again.

____ d. The knight fell in love with the princess.

____ e. The knight killed a dragon with a noose.

____ f. The knight forgot to shine his armor.

____ g. The knight killed a dragon with poison.

Making inferences

C Answer the questions.

1. Why do you think the princess tells the knight not to use his sword?
2. Why does the knight feel unworthy of the town's admiration?
3. Why does the knight's depression go away when he helps the woman in distress?
4. Why does the knight never return to the princess?

Relating reading to personal experience

D Answer these questions.

1. How would you describe the character of the princess? The knight?
2. What is the moral of the story? Do you agree with it?
3. Do you know any women who act like the princess or men who act like the knight? If so, who are they?

MEN, WOMEN, AND SPORTS

1 Available on television night and day, seven days a week, sports is a major part of American television programming. Tens of millions of Americans regularly watch the national broadcasts of major sporting events, although men outnumber women in the viewing audience. Moreover, along with action-adventure and suspense programs, men prefer watching sports while women would rather watch general dramas, situation comedies, variety shows, and soap operas. Given these differences, it is not surprising that men and women will approach, experience, and respond to the same sports program in different ways. In telephone interviews with 707 adults, Walter Gantz, Ph.D., and Lawrence Wenner, Ph.D., found that:

a Men expressed considerably more interest in television sports (51 percent of the men and 24 percent of the women said they were interested). Men were also more likely than women to suffer if sports were taken off television (54 percent to 34 percent would miss it within a week).

b Men spend more time than women watching the sports segment of local newscasts, reading the sports section of newspapers, and talking about sports on a regular basis. Over 50 percent of the male viewers rated themselves "very knowledgeable" about sports, versus 18 percent of females.

c Men watch sports to relax, follow a favorite team, see athletic drama, get psyched up, let off steam, and have something to talk about.

d Women, on the other hand, are more likely to watch for companionship. They join friends and family who are already watching. Thus, it gives women something to do with their friends or family.

e While viewing, men typically talk about the game, yell out in response to action, down snacks and drinks, and put off household chores.

f Women usually work as they watch, and limit their intake of junk food.

g Men are more likely to watch post-game news coverage or follow the action in the newspaper. A winning team puts men in a good mood and prompts them to want to celebrate the victory. But a losing team sometimes puts men in a bad mood, and they avoid their families for a while until they recover.

2 In addition, Walter Stipp, Ph.D., suggests that while men tend to focus more on the moment of victory and defeat, women show "a deeper interest in the athlete and the sport."

3 Still, there are many rabid female sports fans and they act just as their male counterparts do. Gantz, a professor of communications, suspects that in the end, it's the level of "sportsfanship," not gender, that determines TV-viewing behavior.

Adapted from *Journal of Broadcasting & Electronic Media* and *Psychology Today.*

Before you read

Relating to the topic

Check (✔) the statements you think are true.

____ 1. Men watch sports programs on TV more than women do.

____ 2. Men read the sports section of newspapers more than women do.

____ 3. While they watch a game on TV, men work more than women do.

____ 4. While they watch a game on TV, men eat and drink more than women do.

____ 5. While they watch a game on TV, men yell out more than women do.

____ 6. If their team loses, men get more upset than women do.

Reading

Scanning

Scan the text to check your answers. Then read the whole text.

After you read

Understanding figurative language

A Find the words in *italics* in the reading. Then complete the sentences with phrases from the box.

eat or drink	be actively interested in
the opposite of up	the hot gas that is produced when water boils
move along after someone	get rid of energy, anger, or strong emotions

1. a. The common meaning of *steam* is *the hot gas that is produced when water boils*.
   b. The meaning of *let off steam* in par. c is get rid of energy.
2. a. The common meaning of *follow* is move along after s.o.
   b. The meaning of *follow* in par. c is be actively interested.
3. a. The common meaning of *down* is the opposite of up.
   b. The meaning of *down* in par. e is eat or drink.

Understanding details

B What percentage of men and women said these things? Fill in the blanks.

1. *We are sad when there are no sports on TV.*
   a. *54%* of men
   b. 34 of women

2. *We know a lot about sports.*
   a. 50 of men
   b. 18 of women

3. *We are very interested in television sports.*
   a. 51 of men
   b. 24 of women

Relating reading to personal experience

C Answer these questions.

1. How do you react to watching sports ? Is the information in the reading true about you?
2. How would you explain the differences between men's and women's sports-viewing behaviors?
3. In your country, are men or women more interested in sports? Why?

Barefoot in the Park

Paul and Corie live in a tiny apartment with a leaky closet. They've just returned from dinner with a neighbor, where they ate unusual food, such as "knichis" and "poofla-poo pie." Paul is conservative, but Corie is more adventurous. Recently she walked barefoot in the park in cold weather.

PAUL (*Reflectively*) I'm not going to listen to this . . . I'm not going to listen . . . (*He starts for the bedroom*) I've got a case in court in the morning.

CORIE (*Moves left*) Where are you going?

PAUL To sleep.

CORIE Now? How can you sleep now?

PAUL (*Steps up on the bed and turns back, leaning on the door jamb*) I'm going to close my eyes and count knichis. Good night!

CORIE You can't go to sleep now. We're having a fight.

PAUL You have the fight. When you're through, turn off the lights. (*He turns back into the bedroom*)

CORIE Ooh, that gets me insane. You can *even* control your emotions.

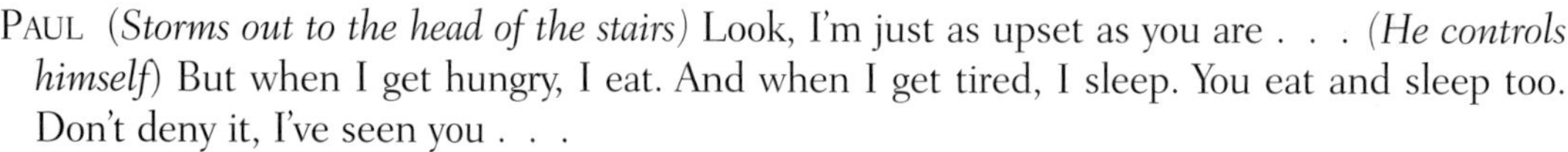

PAUL (*Storms out to the head of the stairs*) Look, I'm just as upset as you are . . . (*He controls himself*) But when I get hungry, I eat. And when I get tired, I sleep. You eat and sleep too. Don't deny it, I've seen you . . .

CORIE (*Moves right with a grand gesture*) Not in the middle of a crisis.

PAUL What crisis? We're just yelling a little.

CORIE You don't consider this a crisis? Our whole marriage hangs in the balance.

PAUL (*Sits on the steps*) It does? When did that happen?

CORIE Just now. It's suddenly very clear that you and I have absolutely *nothing* in common.

PAUL Why? Because I won't walk barefoot in the park in winter? You haven't got a case, Corie.

CORIE (*Seething*) Don't oversimplify this. I'm angry. Can't you see that?

PAUL (*Brings his hands to his eyes, peers at her through imaginary binoculars, and then looks at his watch*) Corie, it's two-fifteen. If I can fall asleep in about half an hour, I can get about five hours' sleep. I'll call you from court tomorrow and we can fight over the phone. (*He gets up and moves to the bedroom*)

CORIE You will *not* go to sleep. You will stay here and fight to save our marriage.

PAUL (*In the doorway*) If our marriage hinges on breathing fish balls and poofla-poo pie, it's not worth saving . . . I am now going to crawl into our tiny, little, single bed. If you care to join me, we will be sleeping from left to right tonight. (*He goes into the bedroom and slams the door*)

CORIE You won't discuss it . . . You're *afraid* to discuss it . . . I married a coward!! . . . (*She takes a shoe from the couch and throws it at the bedroom door*)

PAUL (*Opens the door*) Corie, would you bring in a pail? The closet's dripping.

CORIE Ohh, I hate you! I hate you! I really, really hate you!

PAUL (*Storms to the head of the stairs*) Corie, there is one thing I learned in court. Be careful when you're tired and angry. You might say something you will soon regret. I-am-now-tired-and-angry.

CORIE And a coward.

PAUL (*Comes down the stairs to her at right of the couch*) And I will now say something I will soon regret . . . OK, Corie, maybe you're right. Maybe we have nothing in common. Maybe we rushed into this marriage a little too fast. Maybe love isn't enough. Maybe two people should have to take more than a blood test. Maybe they should be checked for common sense, understanding, and emotional maturity.

Adapted from *Barefoot in the Park.*

Before you read

Predicting

Read the introduction on the opposite page. Who do you think says each statement? Write each statement Paul (*P*) or Corie (*C*).

I'm not going to listen to this.

1. ____

Look, I'm just as upset as you are.

2. ____

It's suddenly very clear that you and I have absolutely nothing in common.

3. ____

You can even control your emotions.

4. ____

Be careful when you're tired and angry.

5. ____

I married a coward!!

6. ____

Reading

Skimming

Skim the text to check your predictions. Then read the whole text.

After you read

Understanding reference words

A What do these words refer to?

1. *this* (line 1) *Corie's complaints*
2. *that* (line 13) ______________
3. *It* (line 20) ______________
4. *this* (line 23) ______________
5. *that* (line 23) ______________
6. *it* (line 29) ______________
7. *it* (line 32) ______________

Making inferences

B Check (✔) the statements that are true.

_✓_ 1. Paul and Corie have not been married for a long time.

____ 2. Corie doesn't have a job.

____ 3. Paul is a lawyer.

____ 4. It is difficult for Corie to control her emotions.

____ 5. Corie thinks Paul is just like his mother.

____ 6. Paul doesn't show his anger easily.

____ 7. Corie and Paul don't always want to do the same things.

Relating reading to personal experience

C Answer these questions.

1. Who do you feel more sympathetic toward, Corie or Paul? Why?
2. Do you think Paul and Corie will have a happy marriage? Why or why not?
3. What do you do when you have a disagreement with someone? Do you say what you're feeling? Or do you try to end the disagreement before you say something you may regret?

Vocabulary expansion

A **Cross out the verb(s) that *cannot* be used with the nouns in *italics*. Use the sample sentences in the dictionary entries below to help you.**

1. *a game*	~~a. do~~	b. watch	c. play	
2. *a good mood*	a. be in	b. have	c. put someone in	
3. *a story*	a. read	b. say	c. tell	d. hear
4. *a test*	a. have	b. show	c. take	d. do
5. *sports*	a. do	b. have	c. play	d. watch
6. *an interest*	a. have	b. make	c. take	d. show
7. *time*	a. go on	b. pass	c. spend	d. waste

game /geɪm/ n an entertaining activity, esp. one played by children, or (a part of) a competition • *The children were playing a game of cops and robbers.* • *I'm going to watch the football game tonight.*

interest /ˈɪn·tər·est/ n the feeling of having your attention held and your mind excited by something or of wanting to be involved with and to discover more about something • *He never seems to show much interest in his children.* • *I've never had any interest in the royal family.* • *She takes more of an interest in politics these days.*

mood /muːd/ n the way you feel at a particular time • *She's in a good mood today.* • *Suddenly her mood changed and she began to ask questions.* • *The music put him in a better mood.*

sport /spɔːrt/ n a game, competition or activity needing physical effort and skill that is played or done according to rules, for enjoyment and/or as a job • *I enjoy watching winter sports like skiing and skating.* • *She used to do a lot of sports when she was younger.* • *Sports that are played indoors include fencing and squash.*

story /ˈstɔːr·i/ n a description, either true or imagined, of a connected series of events and, often, the characters involved in them • *Will you tell me a story?* • *She chose her favorite bedtime story to read the children.* • *He writes children's stories.* • *I've heard that story, but I don't think it's true.*

test /test/ n a way of discovering, by questions or practical activities, what someone knows, or what someone or something can do or is like • *A new driver has to take a driving test.* • *The doctors have done some tests to try and find out what's wrong with her.* • *I can't go out tonight because I have a big test tomorrow.*

time /taɪm/ n a particular period for which something has been happening, or which is needed, or which is available • *If you had taken more time with this essay, you could have done it much better.* • *I've been spending a lot of time at the library.* • *Stop wasting my time with your questions.* • *It's a good way to pass the time while you wait for the bus.*

B **Answer the questions.**

1. Who in your family is good at telling a story?
2. What puts you in a good mood?
3. Do you have any tests this week?
4. Which games do you most like to play?
5. Do you prefer to watch sports or to play sports?
6. Who takes an interest in your improving your English?

Men & women and you

Work in pairs. What stereotypes do people have of men and women? Make lists of ten adjectives often associated with men and ten adjectives often associated with women. Then compare your list with the rest of the class.

UNIT 8 Communication

You are going to read three texts about communication. First, answer the questions in the boxes.

READING 1

Spotting communication problems

Read this magazine article to learn how you can become a more effective communicator and avoid misunderstandings at work.

1. Do you think some people are better communicators than others? If so, what makes them more effective?
2. Where is poor communication a bigger problem — at home, school, or work? Why?

READING 2

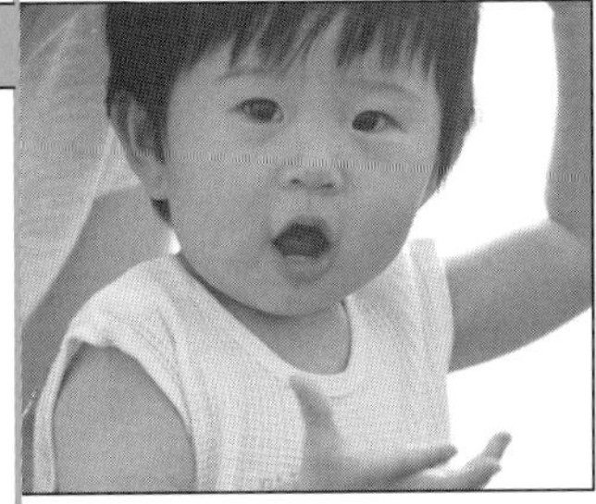

Can babies talk?

This magazine article explains the benefits of babies using signs to communicate.

1. What things do you think a 13-month-old baby wants to say?
2. How do adults usually communicate with a baby before it can speak?

READING 3

Watch your language

What language should parents who come from different countries speak at home? This newspaper article reports one family's solution.

1. What are the advantages of knowing more than one language?
2. Is it confusing for children to learn more than one language when they are young? Why or why not?

Vocabulary

Find out the meanings of the words in the box. Then write each word under the correct heading.

bilingual	broken English	cut someone off	make eye contact
body language	convey a message	get a message across	sign language

RELATED ONLY TO SPEAKING	RELATED TO OTHER COMMUNICATION FORMS
______________________	______________________
______________________	______________________
______________________	______________________
______________________	______________________
______________________	______________________

SPOTTING COMMUNICATION PROBLEMS

1 Are you sometimes slow to communicate with others at work? You may be a *communications laggard*, a term used to describe professionals who perform well in most work areas, but lag behind in their communication skills. If that sounds like you, you're not alone. In fact, a report in the *Wall Street Journal* noted that the single biggest reason people fail to advance in their careers is lack of good communication skills.

2 There are several signs you can use to determine whether you or others are blocking the communication process. Begin by asking yourself whether you are:

- **Using ambiguous body language.** Remember, when you communicate, it's not just the words that convey a message, it's what media experts call "the composite you." This composite takes into account all elements of your body language. For example, if you stand with your back half-turned to someone, if you constantly look away, if your head is lowered, or if you look like you're about to walk away, your body language is sending a signal that you're not interested in having a conversation.
- **Maintaining silent moments.** The next time you have a conversation with a co-worker, make a mental note of how many times you're silent. Periodic silences let people ask questions, acknowledge that they understand what you're saying, and offer ideas of their own.
- **Speaking too fast.** This is one of the most common communication barriers. Conversely, a slow rate of speech implies well-chosen words and strengthens the importance of the message you're conveying. Talking to people in an unhurried manner also gives the listener time to absorb what you have said.
- **Talking with toys.** Do you play with pens, scratch your head, tap your fingers, or clear your throat when you're talking with someone? These mannerisms may be unconscious, but they can be quite annoying to others, who may take you less seriously.
- **Making eye contact.** When you make eye contact, you're telling someone that you're interested in him or her, that you think the person is important, and that you want to hear what he or she has to say.
- **Avoiding overspeak.** Aristotle said, "Think as the wise do, but speak as the common do." Don't use big or obscure words. If others look confused every time you open your mouth, you may be guilty of using "overspeak," a communication barrier that's sure to send people running to the nearest dictionary.
- **Interrupting.** People who cut others off in mid-sentence not only send an unkind message ("I really don't care about what you're saying"), they also cut themselves out of the communication process. Remember that communication is an exchange, and we learn more from listening than from talking.

3 Being a good communicator is a natural skill for only a few people. Most of us have to work at it.

Adapted from *Take Charge Assistant.*

Before you read

Using previous knowledge

How much do you know about communication? Match each poor habit with a resulting problem.

____	1. Speaking too fast	a. annoys other people.
____	2. Playing with pens while talking	b. confuses other people.
____	3. Using unfamiliar words	c. doesn't let the other person speak.
____	4. Interrupting the other person	d. doesn't give people time to follow.

Reading

Skimming

Skim the text to check your answers. Then read the whole text.

After you read

Understanding details

A **Circle the picture that shows good communication skills. For the other pictures, write the part of the article that the man should read.**

1. 

Making eye contact

2. 

____

3. 

____

4. 

____

5. 

____

Restating

B **Compare the meaning of each pair of sentences. Write same (*S*) or different (*D*).**

S 1. If that sounds like you, you're not alone.
There are many people who are similar to you.

____ 2. Lack of communication skills is the main reason for failure to advance.
People's success at work is often dependent upon their communication skills.

____ 3. We learn more from listening than from talking.
How well you listen is often more important than what you say.

____ 4. Most of us have to work at it.
It's easy to improve your communication skills.

Relating reading to personal experience

C **Answer these questions.**

1. Would you rate your communication skills as good, average, or poor?
2. Which skills do you think you should improve?
3. Which parts of the article are true in your culture?

1 Like many 13-month-olds, Brandon knows a few simple words: *mama*, *dada*, and the multipurpose sound *ba* for ball, baby, and bottle. But how can he tell his mother about the hippopotamus at the zoo, the caterpillar in the park, or the piano at Grandma's house? Fortunately for Brandon, his mom has helped him find a way to describe these interesting objects — and many more — even though the words are too difficult for him to say. The solution is what we have come to call baby signs.

2 Similar to the sign language used by the deaf, each baby sign is a simple gesture that stands for a significant object, event, or need in a toddler's world. Just as children learn to wave "bye-bye" long before they can say it, Brandon has learned to open his mouth wide for "hippopotamus," wiggle his finger for "caterpillar," and move his fingers up and down on imaginary keys for "piano." With these and 20 other signs at his disposal, Brandon is able to be an active partner in conversations with the important people in his life. And they, in turn, can appreciate just how much is going on in his mind.

3 "I was absolutely astonished when he walked over to a bench in the park the other day and wiggled his finger, his sign for "caterpillar," recalls Brandon's mother, Lisa. "There was no caterpillar there, but there had been a very big fuzzy one there a few days before. And when I told him that I remembered the caterpillar, too, I could tell from his expression how thrilled he was to have gotten his message across," she says.

4 Baby signs make life with a toddler easier and more fun. Children are less likely to become frustrated, for example, because they can tell you what they want by using signs for "bottle," "wet diaper," and "cold." One toddler invented a sign for "afraid" — patting on his chest repeatedly — and if a dog frightened him, he would add the panting gesture he had learned for "dog" to make the message even clearer. As a result, his family could immediately provide exactly the reassurance he needed: "It's okay, Zack. The doggy is behind the fence."

5 Parents have also been amazed at the way signs open a "window" into their children's minds. Kai, for example, insisted there were alligators in the mall. When his mother let him out of his stroller, he went over to the window of a men's clothing store, proudly pointing to the tiny alligator logos on a rack of men's shirts. If he hadn't known the sign for alligator, his mother would never have appreciated just how observant he was.

6 All in all, baby signs make life sweeter in many ways. Among the additional benefits: higher self-esteem, an increased attention span, greater interest in reading, and closer relationships with older siblings — who seem to find signs enormously entertaining.

Adapted from *Parents*.

Predicting

Before you read

Look at the pictures. What do you think the baby is trying to communicate? Match each picture with a word.

a. b. c.

____ 1. caterpillar ____ 2. hippopotamus ____ 3. piano

Scanning

Reading

Scan the text to check your predictions. Then read the whole text.

After you read

Recognizing audience

A Who do you think the text was written for? Check (✔) the correct answer.

____ 1. college students
__✓__ 3. parents of young children
____ 2. the general public
____ 4. teenagers

Recognizing similarity in meaning

B Match each word or phrase with a word that is similar in meaning.

__c__ 1. *sign* (par. 2) a. *amazed* (par. 5)
__e__ 2. *13-month-old* (par. 1) b. *entertaining* (par. 6)
__d__ 3. *significant* (par. 2) c. *gesture* (par. 2)
__a__ 4. *astonished* (par. 3) d. *important* (par. 2)
__b__ 5. *fun* (par. 4) e. *toddler* (par. 2)

Making inferences

C Check (✔) the statements that are true.

__✓__ 1. Babies can communicate without talking.
____ 2. Using signs will make a baby less interested in learning to speak.
____ 3. Babies will learn signs for whatever their parents teach them.
__✓__ 4. Animals are important in the lives of babies.
__✓__ 5. Baby signs bring a family closer together.

Relating reading to personal experience

D Answer these questions.

1. Would you teach your baby to sign? Why or why not?
2. What signs do you think parents should teach their babies?
3. Think of five signs you could teach a baby. Then see if other students can guess the meanings.

Watch your language

1 My situation is one I could never have imagined: My two very young daughters speak a language I don't. I understand it perfectly, and could, if I had to, keep up a broken version of it. But in our house three languages exist together – English, Spanish, and Catalan. We live in a small village outside Barcelona, where Catalan is the native language of most villagers. I live with Sumpta, my wife, and our two daughters. Julia is four and a half, and Rita is almost two. Julia talks a lot, and Rita is beginning to do the same.

2 One morning I was shaving and Julia was leaning in the bathroom doorway. "Daddy. Mommy speaks English but you don't speak Catalan," she said.

3 "Would you like me to speak Catalan?" I asked.

4 "No!" she said, horrified. "Some daddies speak Catalan, and some don't." Then she turned and shouted downstairs. "Mama, avui vaig al cole?" (Mommy, am I going to school today?)

5 "No! Avui es dissabte!" came the reply. (No, today is Saturday.)

6 "Can I watch a video then?" I could tell by the language that it was me who got to decide this time.

7 "After breakfast."

8 "Aeeeee!" she said.

9 As we went downstairs, I thought back to how we had worried about our three languages before Julia was born.

10 First there was English. Sumpta and I met in English, in England, and we lived in London before moving to Spain. When we moved here, English remained our private language.

11 Sumpta has always used both Catalan and Spanish. Like millions of Catalans, she grew up bilingual.

12 So when Sumpta was pregnant with Julia, we had plenty to think about. I had a fear that my girls would grow up without speaking English. This appeared as a real possibility. I had seen other families, which included foreign parents, who had so assimilated themselves that they had forgotten to pass on their mother tongue until it was too late.

13 We relied heavily on English, our private language, becoming one of Julia's. And because we believed that a language is learned before a child can speak, we talked a lot.

14 So far it has worked. Julia looks at me and speaks English, looks at her mother and speaks Catalan. When she meets a child she doesn't know in the playground, her first words are in Spanish. Rita understands all three, and uses a mixture of words and noises when she speaks. At the moment, Julia speaks to her more in English than Catalan, but it'll be revealing to see which language they choose to speak together as they get older.

15 I have reached the conclusion that adults get much more confused about languages than children. For Julia, the confusion is not that she speaks three languages, but that her father only uses two, and there are some people who restrict themselves to only one.

READING TIP

Words in parentheses sometimes give a translation. For example, note the English translation of the Catalan question in par. 4: "Mama, avui vaig al cole?" (Mommy, am I going to school today?)

Adapted from *The Independent.*

Predicting

Before you read

Read the information about the writer. Then answer the questions below.

The writer is English. His wife is Spanish. They live outside Barcelona with their two daughters. Barcelona is the capital of Catalonia, an autonomous region of Spain, where people speak Spanish and Catalan, but the native language of many people is Catalan.

1. What language do you think the writer speaks to his wife?
2. What language do you think the writer speaks to his children?

Scanning

Reading

Scan the text to check your predictions. Then read the whole text.

Understanding reference words

After you read

A What do these words refer to?

1. *it* (par. 1, line 4) *the language that the writer's daughters speak*
2. *do the same* (par. 1, line 16) ______
3. *the language* (par. 6, line 2) ______
4. *we* (par. 12, line 2) ______
5. *all three* (par. 14, line 8) ______
6. *one* (par. 15, line 9) ______

Understanding details

B Mark the sentences true (T), false (F), or does not give the information (?).

T 1. The writer and his wife are happy that their children speak several languages.
____ 2. Sumpta speaks to her father in Spanish.
____ 3. The writer doesn't speak or understand Catalan.
____ 4. The writer doesn't speak Spanish.
____ 5. Julia is upset because her parents don't speak to her in the same language.
____ 6. If Julia asks a question in English, the writer knows she wants him to answer.
____ 7. The writer knows other families in which the children speak three languages.
____ 8. Julia thinks it's strange that some people speak only one language.

Relating reading to personal experience

C Answer these questions.

1. What are the advantages of speaking to children in different languages? The disadvantages?
2. Do you agree that adults get much more confused about languages than children? Why or why not?
3. If you could have learned another language as a child, which language would you have chosen? Why?

Vocabulary expansion

A **Complete the chart with the missing words.**

	Adjective	Noun	Verb
1.	*acknowledged*	acknowledgment	acknowledge
2.	amazing	amazement	
3.		appreciation	appreciate
4.	astonishing		astonish
5.		avoidance	avoid
6.	communicative	communication	
7.	fallible		fail
8.	imaginary		imagine
9.	observant		observe
10.	performing		perform
11.	reassuring	reassurance	
12.	significant	significance	

B **Read the sentences. Write the part of speech of the missing word. Then complete the sentences with the correct words from the chart.**

1. People who are *communicative* (*adj.*) are better able to work with the public.
2. People ______________ each other's body language when they are talking to each other. For example, they watch each other closely to pick up non-verbal clues.
3. Many people are afraid of ______________ and avoid speaking before an audience. They think they won't do a good job.
4. When people are afraid to speak in public, it's important to ______________ them. They need support to build their confidence.
5. Audiences are ______________ when speakers speak clearly because they can understand the speaker better.
6. Poor communication skills affect people's ______________ at work and at school. They can't acheive as much as they want to.
7. Common communication mistakes are ______________ if people learn some simple rules.

Communication and you

Give a 2-minute speech on a subject of your choice. Your classmates will evaluate your performance. They will pay attention to your use of some of the communication skills presented in "Spotting communication problems," including rate of speech, eye contact with your audience, nervous habits, and appropriate body language.

UNIT 9 Dishonesty

You are going to read three texts about dishonesty. First, answer the questions in the boxes.

READING 1

The telltale signs of lying

Can you recognize when someone is lying to you? This magazine article describes clues to determine whether someone is telling the truth or a lie.

1. Do you know anyone who often tells lies? If so, who is it?
2. Why do you think people lie?

READING 2

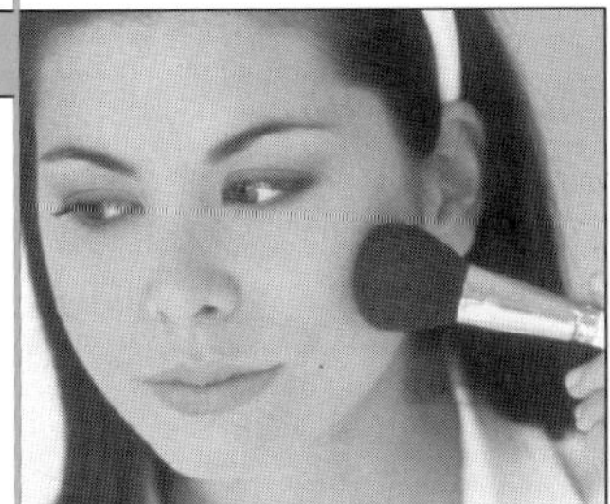

If it sounds too good to be true . . .

Advertisers often make misleading statements about products. This newspaper article investigates the facts behind some advertisements.

1. What advertisement have you seen recently that you like? Why? What claims did the ad make about its product?
2. Do you usually believe what advertisements say? Why or why not?

READING 3

Truth or consequences

Are students cheating more nowadays than in the past? Read this newspaper article about cheating in schools today.

1. Why do you think some students cheat?
2. What are the consequences of cheating in your country?

Vocabulary

Find out the meanings of the words in *italics*. Then answer the questions.

1. Do you think that *deception* is ever acceptable?
2. Have you ever *challenged* someone you thought was lying?
3. Do you know anyone who makes *contradictory* statements?
4. Do you think most advertising *claims* are true?
5. Have you ever *created a false impression* about what you could do?

The telltale **signs of lying**

1 Psychologists tell us that lying is a characteristic human behavior and happens for two reasons: to receive rewards and/or to avoid punishment. Whether we lie depends on our calculation of the rewards and punishment.

2 This is called "situational honesty." Because most of us are trained to believe lying is wrong, it creates stress. (That's not true with very young children and pathological liars — people who cannot control their lying because of a psychological problem.)

3 When under stress, a person who is lying normally displays several verbal and nonverbal clues. Most of the verbal clues will be obvious when the individual is asked a difficult question. For example, consider the case of Delbert, an employee of a large company. Because of labor problems, the director started receiving threatening letters from a company worker. Clues had led to one department with about a dozen workers. Delbert was interviewed first. During the interview, he had several reactions typical of liars. Here are two of them.

4 **Repetition of the question**

Q: Do you know why anyone would write the director a threatening note?

A: Do I know why anyone would write the director a threatening note?

Liars frequently repeat a question, gaining time to think of a false answer.

Selective memory

Q: Do you remember whether you were working on the date this last letter was mailed?

A: I might have been working, or I might have been off; I just don't remember.

5 If Delbert had been the writer, he would know very well where he was when the letter was mailed. But he gave a vague answer to avoid being caught in a lie.

6 The nonverbal clues of deception are also obvious. When threatened, humans react with a "fight or flight" mentality. Thus, when dealing with stress, the body has trouble remaining still. Some people, when asked difficult questions, subconsciously adopt a position as if they were about to leave the room suddenly. This happened with Delbert. While his head was facing me, his feet were pointed in the direction of the door as if he were ready to rush from the room.

7 Another way to relieve stress through movement is to change positions. When we were talking, Delbert remained relatively motionless. But when I asked him a difficult question, he visibly shifted his position in the chair, moving his whole body in the process.

8 A similar reaction to stress involves crossing motions. When people feel threatened, they can subconsciously use their arms for protection. I noticed that in response to some questions, Delbert crossed his arms as if to protect himself from attack.

9 It may seem childish, but some liars cover their mouths when telling a lie. That's because in times of stress, many people instinctively revert to their childhood emotions. Delbert frequently covered his mouth with his hand as if his lie would escape.

10 Regardless of the reason for lying, there's a valuable lesson in this interview. If you observe and listen carefully, you can improve your ability to recognize lies.

Adapted from *Journal of Accountancy*.

Before you read

Relating to the topic

Check (✔) the clues you think a person displays when telling a lie.

____	1. repeating a question	____	5. responding clearly to questions
____	2. speaking in a softer voice	____	6. answering a question with a question
____	3. making direct eye contact	____	7. forgetting important details
____	4. changing body positions	____	8. covering the mouth with a hand

Reading

Scanning

Scan the text to check your answers. Then read the whole text.

After you read

Understanding details

A Check (✔) the answer that best completes each statement.

1. People lie

____ a. to make themselves look better.

_✓_ b. to get benefits for themselves.

____ c. to improve their social position.

2. The director received threatening letters

____ a. because there were financial problems in the company.

_✓_ b. because there were labor problems in the company.

____ c. because there were management problems in the company.

3. Delbert seemed to be lying because

____ a. his handwriting matched the writing in the letters.

____ b. he often contradicted himself during the interview.

_✓_ c. his physical and verbal behavior were typical of liars.

Guessing meaning from context

B Find the words in *italics* in the reading. Circle the meaning of each word.

1. *telltale* (title)	(a.) showing information	b. keeping information secret
2. *situational* (par. 2)	a. based on a belief	b. based on what is happening
3. *nonverbal* (pars. 3, 6)	a. without spoken language	b. using exactly the same words
4. *selective* (par. 4)	a. having many choices	b. choosing only some things
5. *fight or flight* (par. 6)	a. angry or irresponsible	b. facing or escaping danger
6. *subconsciously* (pars. 6, 8)	a. without being aware	b. showing interest or worry

Relating reading to personal experience

C Answer these questions.

1. Would you confront someone you thought was lying to you? Why or why not?
2. Do you agree that lying is a characteristic human behavior? Why or why not?
3. Can you think of other clues that reveal when a person is lying? If so, what are they?

If it sounds too good to be true . . .

1 Are your paper towels honestly the most absorbent money can buy? Do physicians truly prefer your pain medication to all others? Will your makeup really not rub off on your clothes? Well, that's what the ads say.

2 Advertising claims are everywhere, but it's not enough to say that your paper towels are the most absorbent. Unless it's really true, there's a good chance someone – especially a competitor – is going to make you prove it. It's a little-known fact of business life, but advertising is challenged all the time. One of the leading judges of such challenges is the national advertising division of the Council of Better Business Bureau. For over 30 years, the organization's advertising experts have examined the wording in ads to answer such questions as: Is it true that ColorStay makeup "won't rub off on your collar"?

3 To test this claim, a leading competitor asked hundreds of women to wear white shirts, spend the day doing what they usually do, and wear ColorStay makeup. The company wanted to test ColorStay's claim for itself.

4 The competitor claimed that its results showed that ColorStay makeup actually does rub off. But ColorStay's manufacturer also conducted its own test on hundreds of women. Its results were the opposite. The testers found that the makeup stayed on during normal use.

5 The contradictory tests impressed the Council of Better Business Bureau's advertising division. It concluded that the questions came down to how viewers would interpret the word "rub." It decided that ColorStay's manufacturer had proved the makeup effectively resists rubbing off during "normal use." The company revised its advertising claim to include the words "under normal conditions."

6 The advertising division of the Council of Better Business Bureau was created in 1971 by advertisers in the U.S. as a way to regulate themselves. Since then, numerous cases have come to the advertising division to show how a truth – improperly presented – can create the wrong impression.

7 This was the finding regarding the TV commercial for a new brand of pain medication, Orudis KT. The ad claimed: "There are many prescription pain medications, and a doctor can prescribe any of them. Yet, 82 percent of doctors surveyed have prescribed Orudis."

8 Literally true, the advertising division decided. The doctors had prescribed Orudis at least once during their lifetimes. The advertising division concluded, however, that the way the statement was worded created the false impression that doctors had chosen Orudis over other pain medication.

9 The manufacturer objected to the decision, though it agreed to take the advertising divisions comments into account in its future advertising of Orudis KT. It noted that the company had already discontinued the ads.

Adapted from *Minneapolis Star Tribune.*

Before you read

Predicting

Read the first paragraph on the opposite page. Then check (✔) the information you think you will read about in the text.

____ 1. examples of misleading ads

____ 2. examples of honest ads

____ 3. competitors' reactions to ads

____ 4. organizations that judge the honesty of ads

Reading

Scanning

Scan the text to check your predictions. Then read the whole text.

After you read

Understanding reference words

A What do these words refer to?

1. *it* (par. 2, line 5) *the claim that your paper towels are the most absorbent*
2. *this claim* (par. 3, line 1) ____
3. *Its* (par. 4, line 6) ____
4. *It* (par. 5, line 7) ____
5. *the statement* (par. 8, line 7) ____

Understanding details

B Mark each sentence true (*T*) or false (*F*).

____ 1. People who have bought a company's products most often challenge its ads.

____ 2. The ColorStay ad claimed that women wouldn't get the makeup on their clothes.

____ 3. The manufacturer of ColorStay did tests that found its ad was true.

____ 4. A competitor of ColorStay did tests that found the ColorStay ad was untrue.

____ 5. The advertising division of the Council of Better Business Bureau decided that the ColorStay ad was completely false.

____ 6. After the advertising division gave its opinion of the ad, the manufacturer of ColorStay changed its ad.

____ 7. Eighty-two percent of doctors prescribed Orudis pain medication at least once.

____ 8. Eighty-two percent of doctors preferred Orudis to other pain medications.

Relating reading to personal experience

C Answer these questions.

1. Have you ever seen a misleading advertisement? If so, what was it?
2. Do you think it is important to regulate advertisers? Why or why not?
3. Do you consider an advertiser's claims when choosing a product? What else do you consider?

Truth or consequences

1 What's the most creative technique for cheating that you know? At one American high school, Ivan Baumwell watched a friend print out the answers to a history test in tiny type and tape them inside her water bottle. Devon Watts pried apart her watch before an exam and slid a cheat sheet in front of the watch face. Lindsey Kleidman's classmates took tissues from their teacher's desk during a math test, so they could read the answer key upside down. But one method stood out from all the rest: Trevor Snell says he watched another student take advantage of his school's eating-in-class policy by hollowing out an apple and stuffing the answers to a physics test inside.

2 These students were among the dozens across the country who talked about their experiences with cheating. Everyone interviewed said that cheating was widespread in his or her school. The majority admitted cheating at some point themselves. Does that mean that their schools are isolated academic disaster areas? Hardly, according to a disturbing new report on cheating. It just makes them typical.

3 A national survey of 8,600 students released by Michael Josephson of the Josephson Institute of Ethics reveals what a cheating-happy culture high school has become: 71 percent of American teenagers admitted cheating on at least one exam within the last year, up from 60 percent ten years earlier; and 78 percent said they'd lied to a teacher.

4 So why is the United States becoming a nation of cheaters? Is pressure to succeed at any cost taking the place of pride in one's accomplishments? Are too many teachers asleep at the wheel? Every student we spoke with has his or her own explanation. The only thing they all agreed on was that cheating is everywhere.

5 Kent Petrino, 17, blames clueless teachers. "They need to pay more attention if they want to stop students from cheating," he says. "A lot of kids are really obvious about cheating because they know they can get away with it."

6 Teachers, not surprisingly, reject this excuse. "It's true some teachers are oblivious," says Kent's teacher, Judy Carrico. "But our job is to teach, not to police every student. I really think parents have to instill this in their kids. And kids need to monitor themselves. We have so much to do, we can't do it for them."

7 Yet students still do it and risk punishments including parental notification, suspension, and even an automatic failing grade. Are there any additional long-term consequences? "Of course there are," says Laura Mills, 17. "Cheaters are just cheating themselves out of skills they need. I had to test out for my lifeguard training. If I'd cheated on my test, I wouldn't be prepared to deal with life-and-death decisions."

8 Josephson agrees. "Do we really want the next generation of paramedics and airplane pilots and nuclear-missile designers to be people who cheated their way through school?" he asks.

READING TIP

When people are quoted, their first and last names are given the first time they appear. After that, only the first or last name appears. For example, "Kent Petrino" is later identified only as "Kent."

Adapted from *The New York Times Upfront.*

Before you read

Using previous knowledge

How much do you know about cheating? Circle the information you think is correct.

1. Cheating in schools is **more** / **less** common nowadays than in the past.
2. Cheating happens in **all** / **some** schools.
3. **A lot of** / **Only a few** students lie to their teacher.
4. Students cheat because **exams are difficult** / **cheating is easy**.
5. When students cheat, there are **few** / **many** serious consequences.

Reading

Scanning

Scan the text to check your answers. Then read the whole text.

After you read

Understanding details

A **Number the pictures in the order they are mentioned, from 1 (first) to 4 (last). (Be careful! There is one extra picture.)**

____ a.

____ b.

__1__ c.

____ d.

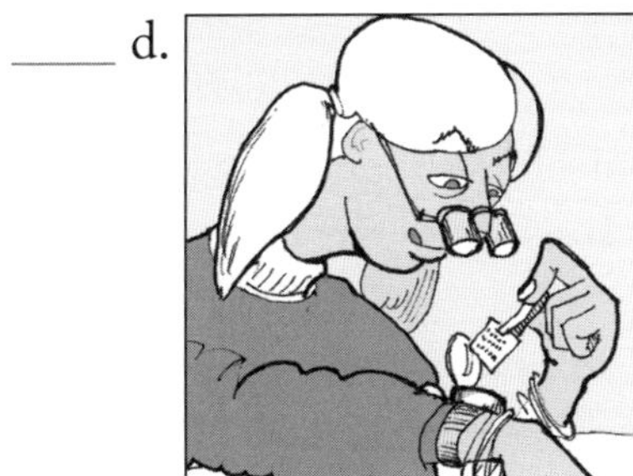

____ e.

Recognizing tone

B **What is the tone of the text? Check (✔) the correct answer.**

____ 1. angry

____ 2. funny

____ 3. sad

____ 4. serious

Relating reading to personal experience

C **Answer these questions.**

1. What other cheating techniques have you heard of?
2. What do you think should be done to reduce cheating?
3. What would you do if a student who cheated on a test got a higher score than you?

Vocabulary expansion

A **Look at these words from previous units. Circle the words in which *dis-* means *opposite of*. Cross out the words in which *dis-* does not have that meaning.**

1. discontinue	5. disagree	9. dislike
~~2. disaster~~	6. disappear	10. disposal
3. disabled	7. discover	11. disturbing
4. disadvantage	8. discuss	12. distress

B **Answer the questions.**

1. Are you satisfied or dissatisfied with your understanding of this unit?
2. Do you usually show interest or disinterest when your teacher explains something?
3. Were you pleased or displeased with the last grade you got?
4. Do people think you're organized or disorganized?
5. When you were little, did you always obey your parents, or did you sometimes disobey them?
6. Is your bedroom in a state of order or disorder?
7. Have your parents always approved of what you've done, or have they sometimes disapproved?
8. Do you have a feeling of comfort or discomfort when you give a speech?

Dishonesty and you

Make three statements about yourself, only one of which is true. Your classmates will vote on which statement is true. If you fool the class, you win and become a member of the "Liar's Club."

UNIT 10 Etiquette

You are going to read three texts about etiquette. First, answer the questions in the boxes.

READING 1

Cell phone yakkers need manners

Do cell phone users sometimes annoy you? This newspaper article explores a growing problem around the world.

1. Do you have a cell phone? If so, when and where do you use it?
2. What should people do to avoid disturbing others when they use cell phones?

READING 2

How table manners became polite

This newspaper article describes how our ideas about table manners have changed over the centuries.

1. Does your family have any special rules for manners at meal times? If so, what are they?
2. Do other people's table manners sometimes bother you? If so, which ones?

READING 3

Dinner with my parents

Inviting a boyfriend or girlfriend to have a meal with your parents is always a risk. Read this book excerpt to find out what happened at one such meal.

1. How often does your family invite guests for a meal? What do you do differently when you have guests?
2. Have you ever had an embarrassing experience while eating in someone else's home? If so, what happened?

Vocabulary

Find out the meanings of the words in *italics*. Then answer the questions.

1. If a student doesn't show *courtesy* to others, what should the teacher do?
2. What is an example of bad table *manners*?
3. Should a student be *offended* if the teacher does not remember his or her name?
4. How can you be *thoughtful* when you use a cell phone?
5. What is an example of *rude* classroom behavior?
6. Should a teacher *decline* an invitation to have a meal with a student?

Cell phone yakkers need manners

1 With a cell phone glued to her ear, Deirdre — as she announced herself to a succession of people she was calling — sat in the crowded airport, talking loudly about her day-care troubles, her family, and her mother's surgery.

2 For those sitting near her, there was no way to ignore this modern-day scourge: the public cell phone yakker who talks about private matters in front of unwilling listeners.

3 When someone nearby finally asked her to take her next private conversation elsewhere, it was Deirdre who was offended:

4 "That's the rudest thing I've ever heard."

5 As cell phone users continue to yak away in public, the matter of who is being rude has opened a national discussion over cell phone etiquette — or lack thereof.

6 Mary Mitchell, author of five books on etiquette, said: "We are overhearing conversations we should not be overhearing, even though we don't want to be overhearing them."

7 It is hard to block out cell phone talkers, who unknowingly tend to speak louder than they would to someone face-to-face. So people are overhearing one-sided conversations on marital breakups, business deals, and what's for dinner.

8 Those who operate museums, movie theaters, schools, restaurants, and parks are struggling to limit annoying uses of cell phones. Communities and states are also examining whether to limit cell phone use by drivers for safety reasons.

9 Remember telephone booths? They were created with the idea that only the person you were calling should hear what you were saying. That's still a useful concept to keep in mind when using your cell phone.

10 Below are some basic rules for cell phone etiquette:

- Use your cell phone in public only when necessary.
- If you are not expecting an urgent call, turn off the phone during business meetings, at social gatherings, in restaurants, and at the theater. In these situations, rely on your beeper if you have one, and set the beeper to vibrate mode.
- If you absolutely must keep your phone on during a meeting, explain in advance.
- If you must make a call at a social gathering or at a restaurant, excuse yourself and find a reasonably private space in which to make the call.
- If you must speak while others are near, speak softly. Your conversation may be fascinating to you, but it's of no interest to others.
- If you use your cell phone while driving, you deserve whatever happens. Others do not. Pull over and take the few minutes you need to make your call.

Adapted from *The Ottawa Citizen.*

Before you read

Relating to the topic

Check (✔) the statements you agree with.

_____ 1. Cell phone users rarely talk about private matters in public places.

_____ 2. If someone using a cell phone is disturbing you, it's best not to do anything.

_____ 3. The use of cell phones forces people to overhear the conversations of others.

_____ 4. People speak more loudly on cell phones than in ordinary conversation.

_____ 5. We should have laws that limit cell phone use while driving.

_____ 6. It's OK to use a cell phone in a restaurant if you speak softly.

Reading

Scanning

Scan the text to find out which statements the writer agrees with. Then read the whole text.

After you read

Guessing meaning from context

A Find the words in *italics* in the reading. Circle the meaning of each word.

1. A *succession of people* means **the people are very successful** / **one person after another.** (par. 1)
2. If something is a *scourge*, it causes people a lot of **sadness** / **trouble.** (par. 2)
3. A *yakker* is **someone who talks a lot** / **someone who uses a cell phone.** (par. 2)
4. If people are *unwilling* to do something, they **want** / **don't want** to do it. (par. 2)
5. To *block out* something means to **move away from** / **ignore** it. (par. 7)
6. To *operate* something means to **go to** / **manage** it. (par. 8)
7. If something *vibrates*, you **hear** / **feel** it. (par. 10)

Summarizing

B Check (✔) the best summary of the article.

_____ 1. The article describes what cell phone users can do to avoid disturbing others.

_____ 2. The article gives examples of the rudeness of some cell phone users.

_____ 3. The article discusses the rudeness of some cell phone users and gives advice on improving cell phone manners.

Relating reading to personal experience

C Answer these questions.

1. What do you do when you are in public and someone with a cell phone disturbs you?
2. Where should cell phones be allowed? Where should they *not* be allowed?
3. What advice in the article do you agree with? What do you disagree with?

How table manners became polite

1 If you don't like having to sit up straight and keep your elbows off the table, be grateful you weren't a child of America's early settlers. Back then, children didn't even get to sit at the table. They stood behind the adults and ate whatever the adults gave them.

2 Later, children were allowed to sit at the table, but they couldn't speak unless an adult spoke to them. They couldn't ask for a dish, either. They had to wait until a grownup offered it to them. It was also considered rude to fidget, sing, or look at someone else who was eating.

3 Table manners are even older than tables. About 9,000 years ago, people cooked soups in pots. They dipped spoons of wood or bone into the cooking pot to eat. Sometimes they didn't use spoons, they just picked out pieces of meat with their fingers.

4 Eating with the fingers has never disappeared. Some cultures still follow this custom. Certain groups use only the first three fingers of the right hand. In northern India, some diners use only the fingertips of the right hand, but in the south, using both hands is okay. In fact, far more people eat with fingers or chopsticks than use forks and spoons. But everyone has rules about eating politely.

5 Table manners became quite important in Europe in the 1100s. That's when people developed the idea of courtesy, or how to behave in court. Soon these rules began appearing in written texts.

6 The rules about eating were meant to make the experience pleasant, thoughtful, and tidy. Early texts instructed diners to keep their elbows down and not to speak with their mouths full. Polite diners were not to pick their teeth with their knives or be greedy.

7 In those days, people didn't have regular dining tables. At mealtimes, wooden boards were laid out and covered with cloth, therefore the expression "setting the table." At banquets, no individual plates were used, only large serving platters. Two people shared each soup bowl and used squares of stale bread as plates. These edible plates were called trenchers. After the meal, they were given to the poor.

8 In the 1300s, the Renaissance arrived. So did the fork. As new table customs evolved, people began to eat from plates, and everyone had his own cup. Fingers were to be wiped on napkins, not tablecloths. Bones were not to be thrown on the floor, but left on the plate. Manners kept moving toward cleanliness and order.

9 Nowadays people use many simple table manners without thinking. You probably say "please" and "thank you," and ask for food to be passed to you, rather than reaching over everyone for it.

10 There are many other rules, especially in more formal settings, such as parties, where you're supposed to use the right fork. If you are not sure what to do, just watch the host or hostess and do what he or she does. Even if you use the wrong fork, you'll be following the basic principle of table manners: Think about others and make dining as pleasant as possible.

Adapted from *The Christian Science Monitor.*

Before you read

Thinking about personal experience

Check (✔) the table manners that are polite in your country.

____ 1. sitting up straight

____ 2. keeping your elbows off the table

____ 3. not looking at someone else who is eating

____ 4. using your right hand to eat

____ 5. speaking with food in your mouth

____ 6. picking your teeth

____ 7. using a napkin to wipe your hands

____ 8. saying "please" and "thank you"

Reading

Skimming

Skim the text and check (✔) the main idea of the article. Then read the whole text.

____ 1. The main idea is the history of table manners.

____ 2. The main idea is the rules of eating around the world.

____ 3. The main idea is the reasons for modern table manners.

After you read

Recognizing audience

A Who do you think the text was written for? Check (✔) the correct answer.

____ 1. people all over the world

____ 2. people who eat with chopsticks

____ 3. people who eat with knives and forks

____ 4. people who eat with their hands

Restating and making inferences

B Check (✔) the correct column.

	Inference	Restatement	Not in the text
1. Family life was very strict in early America.	✓		
2. Children in early America were often hungry.			
3. People started using spoons thousands of years ago.			
4. All over the world, there are rules about eating.			
5. Before the 1100s in Europe, table manners were not very important.			
6. In Europe in the 1300s, there were many changes in table manners.			

Relating reading to personal experience

C Answer these questions.

1. What rules about table manners does a visitor to your country need to know?
2. How important are table manners? Do you think people should be able to eat however they want?
3. Do you like people less when they have poor table manners? Why or why not?

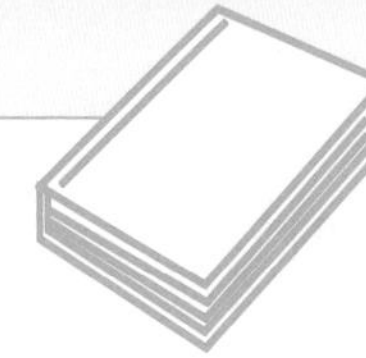

Dinner with my parents

Amy Tan (1952 -) *Tan's novels pay particular attention to ethnicity, family history, and the importance of female voices.*

1 I couldn't save Rich in the kitchen. And I couldn't save him later at the dinner table.

2 When I offered Rich a fork, he insisted on using his slippery ivory chopsticks. He held them splayed like the knock-kneed legs of an ostrich while picking up a large chunk of sauce-coated eggplant. Halfway between his plate and his open mouth, the chunk fell on his crisp white shirt. It took several minutes to get Shoshana to stop shrieking with laughter.

3 And then he had helped himself to big portions of the shrimp and snow peas, not realizing he should have taken only a polite spoonful, until everybody had had a morsel.

4 He had declined the sautéed new greens, the tender and expensive leaves of bean plants plucked before the sprouts turn into beans. And Shoshana refused to eat them also, pointing to Rich: "He didn't eat them! He didn't eat them!"

5 He thought he was being polite by refusing seconds, when he should have followed my father's example, who made a big show of taking small portions of seconds, thirds, and even fourths, always saying he could not resist another bite of something or other, and then groaning that he was so full he thought he would burst.

6 But the worst was when Rich criticized my mother's cooking, and he didn't even know what he had done. As is the Chinese cook's custom, my mother always made disparaging remarks about her own cooking. That night she chose to direct it toward her famous steamed pork and preserved vegetable dish, which she always served with special pride.

7 "Ai! This dish not salty enough, no flavor," she complained, after tasting a small bit. "It is too bad to eat."

8 This was our family's cue to eat some and proclaim it the best she had ever made. But before we could do so, Rich said, "You know, all it needs is a little soy sauce." And he proceeded to pour a riverful of the salty black stuff on the platter, right before my mother's horrified eyes.

9 And even though I was hoping throughout the dinner that my mother would somehow see Rich's kindness, his sense of humor and boyish charm, I knew he had failed miserably in her eyes.

READING TIP

Words in English can have many meanings. Do not assume that you know which meaning is intended. For example, in this text, *seconds*, *thirds*, and *fourths* refer to extra servings of food (that is, a second serving, a third serving, and a fourth serving).

Adapted from *The Joy Luck Club*.

Before you read

Predicting

Read the information below. Then check (✔) what you think will happen.

In this excerpt from The Joy Luck Club, *Waverly takes her American boyfriend, Rich, to meet her parents. Her daughter, Shoshana, also comes with them. Waverly's parents were born in China, but they live in California.*

____ 1. Waverly's parents' table manners will surprise Rich.

____ 2. Waverly's parents and Rich will talk about the differences between American and Chinese table manners.

____ 3. Rich's behavior will be acceptable to Americans, but rude in the Chinese culture.

Reading

Scanning

Scan the text to check your prediction. Then read the whole text.

After you read

Understanding details

A **What advice could Waverly have given Rich? Complete the sentences.**

1. Don't use _chopsticks_ if you don't know how to hold them properly. (par. 2)
2. Take a ________ portion of food to start with. (par. 3)
3. ________ everything. (par. 4)
4. Don't refuse ________ . (par. 5)
5. Don't ________ the cook. (par. 6)

Understanding complex sentences

B **Separate each sentence from the text into two or three new sentences.**

1. (par. 3) And then he had helped himself to _big portions of the shrimp and snow peas_ .
   He didn't realize that _he should have taken only a polite spoonful_ .
2. (par. 5) He thought he was being polite by ________ .
   However, he should have ________ .
   My father made ________ .
   He always said ________ .
   Then he groaned ________ .
3. (par. 9) I hoped throughout the dinner that my mother ________ .
   However, I knew ________ .

Relating reading to personal experience

C **Answer these questions.**

1. What do you think Waverly and Rich said about the dinner the next day? How about Waverly's parents?
2. Do you think Rich should apologize to Waverly's parents? Why or why not?
3. Have you ever used the wrong table manners? If so, what happened?

Vocabulary expansion

A **Look at how the ending *–ful* can be used. Then check (✔) the correct column for each word below.**

The ending *-ful* can mean the amount something can hold.
He should have taken only a polite *spoonful.*
He proceeded to pour a *riverful* of the salty black stuff on the platter.
The ending *-ful* can also refer to a characteristic someone or something has.
That's still a *useful* concept to keep in mind.
A *thoughtful* diner will try to make the experience pleasant for others.

	An amount	A characteristic		An amount	A characteristic
1. useful		✓	7. mouthful		
2. spoonful	✓		8. peaceful		
3. cheerful			9. roomful		
4. handful			10. powerful		
5. helpful			11. successful		
6. hopeful			12. thankful		

B **Complete each sentence with a word from exercise A.**

1. I usually put one _spoonful_ of sugar in my tea.
2. Our neighbors were very ________ that we had helped them.
3. She was a ________ hostess who always smiled when she had visitors.
4. There was a ________ of twenty or thirty guests.
5. Our party on Saturday was so ________ that we might have another one soon.
6. Everything was ________ until the teenagers started fighting.
7. The little girl gave her grandmother a ________ of flowers from the garden.

Etiquette and you

Work in pairs. Choose one of these situations. Make a list of what foreign visitors to your country should know about proper etiquette in the situation you have chosen.

Weddings	Business	Dinner parties
invitations	appointments	invitations
the ceremony	entertainment	seating arrangements
the reception	gifts	tableware
gifts	letter writing	who is served first and last

UNIT 11 Love

You are going to read three texts about love. First, answer the questions in the boxes.

READING 1

True love is over in 30 months

Do you think love is forever? Find out what some scientists report in this newspaper article.

1. Do you believe love can last forever? Why do you think many relationships don't last?
2. Who do you think fall in love more easily — men or women?

READING 2

Choosing a dog is like falling in love

This newspaper article describes the similarities between the dogs we like and the people we fall in love with.

1. Why do people like dogs as pets?
2. Do you have (or have you ever had) a dog? What do (or did) you like about the dog?

READING 3

Love Song for Lucinda; Ashes of Life

Read what two poets write about love.

1. How does love make people feel? What are some problems people have when they fall in love?
2. How do people feel when a love relationship ends?

Vocabulary

Find out the meanings of the words and phrases in the box. Then write them on the time line in the order that you think they usually occur.

break up	fall in love	heart goes "pit-a-pat"	romance
court/get courted	fall out of love	love becomes habit	sweaty palms

Beginning of a relationship

1. ________
2. ________
3. ________
4. ________
5. ________
6. ________
7. ________
8. ________

True love is over in 30 months

1 Love is not forever. In fact, for most people, it lasts no more than 30 months. After that, according to one of the world's top researchers into the nature of romance, couples face the choice of breaking up or continuing on out of habit.

2 The conclusions of Professor Cindy Hazan of Cornell University are based on 5,000 interviews across 37 cultures and medical tests on couples. The conclusions challenge the romantic ideal and suggest instead that men and women are biologically and mentally predisposed to be "in love" for only 18–30 months. That is just long enough for a couple to meet, mate, and have a child. After that, there is no evolutionary need for the sweaty palms often associated with the high point of love.

3 "There is mounting evidence that what we call love is created by a chemical cocktail in the brain triggered through social conditioning," says Hazan. These chemicals, which are registered together only during the initial stages of courtship, are dopamine, phenylethylamine, and oxytocin. But even the most ardent romantics develop a tolerance to the effects of these chemicals. "The effect wears off, returning people to a relatively relaxed state of mind within two years," says Hazan.

4 "By that time, couples have either parted or decided that they are easy enough with each other to stay together. Love becomes a habit, especially if children are in the frame. But those chemicals rarely return again in the relationship. That is it for true love."

5 People who need these chemicals could become serial romantics, she says, such as Henry VIII. "They are genuinely in love, or at least the chemicals make them think they are – which amounts to the same thing."

6 The Cornell study indicates that most men fall in love more quickly and easily than women, and that women end most relationships. This may suggest that women get less hooked on the cocktail of love.

7 People can be shocked by how quickly they fall out of love. Actress Gwyneth Paltrow revealed why she left Brad Pitt after nearly three years together. "I was sure Brad was the love of my life and then suddenly one day I did not feel the same. Nothing happened, but doubt set in. I told myself it was better to have enjoyed the relationship while it lasted rather than try to stretch it out and become really unhappy," she said.

8 Yet there are those who get through the 30-month barrier. Jean Wormall, 73, has been married for 54 years. She met Bill in the 1940s, and they had a child after a year of marriage. She said: "It's good for couples to have a year or two together to see if it will really work before having a family. But do not think you can regain that first flush of love. You have to find another word for what keeps you going."

Adapted from *The Sunday Times*.

READING TIP Sometimes knowing something about a subject can help you understand the meaning of a word or phrase. For example, King Henry VIII of England (1509–1547), had six wives. Here, he is described as a "serial romantic" because he fell in love with one woman after another.

Relating to the topic

Before you read

Check (✔) the statements you agree with.

____ 1. Most long-term relationships are based on habit, not on love.

____ 2. Love is caused by chemicals in the brain.

____ 3. Most relationships are ended by men.

____ 4. There is a biological need for long-term relationships.

Scanning

Reading

Scan the text to find out which statements are true. Then read the whole text.

Guessing meaning from context

After you read

A Find the words in *italics* in the reading. Circle the meaning of each word.

1. If you are *predisposed to* something, you are **interested in** / **taught** / **likely to do** it. (par. 2)
2. When something is *mounting*, it **stays the same** / **gets larger** / **gets smaller**. (par. 3)
3. An *ardent* romantic is **bored** / **unhappy** / **enthusiastic**. (par. 3)
4. People who have *parted* have **stayed together** / **left each other** / **fallen in love**. (par. 4)
5. When people are *hooked*, they are **dependent** / **confident** / **finished**. (par. 6)
6. When you *regain* your feeling of love, you **lose it** / **want it** / **get it back**. (par. 8)

Understanding details

B Circle the answer that is *not* true.

1. What does Professor Hazan's research show?
   a. Women do not fall in love as quickly as men do.
   b. Men fall in love more easily than women do.
   c. Chemicals in the brain affect women more than men.
2. Why did Gwyneth Paltrow leave Brad Pitt?
   a. She was feeling really unhappy.
   b. She began to doubt her love for him.
   c. Her feelings for him had changed.
3. What does the text say about Jean Wormall?
   a. She is glad she married Bill, and she loves him more and more each year.
   b. She feels the same way about her husband as she did when she first fell in love.
   c. She loves her husband, but it is not the same kind of love she felt many years ago.

Relating reading to personal experience

C Answer these questions.

1. Which would you prefer — being "out of love" in a long-term relationship or being "in love" in many short-term relationships? Why?
2. How is the information in the article different from how love is usually portrayed in movies, books, and songs?
3. In your culture, is love the most important thing when choosing someone to marry? What else is important?

Choosing a dog is like falling in love

1 Whether we're dancing at a club or playing ball in the park, there are certain looks and personality traits that make the heart go "pit-a-pat." The characteristics that appeal to us in a dog are often the exact ones we seek in a mate. Our choice of significant others and dogs goes paw in hand and it reveals how we view ourselves and the world around us.

2 "Often, we search for another who makes us complete," says Sarah Wilson, co-author of "Good Owners, Great Dogs." And what we feel we are lacking, we seek from our significant others – qualities that make us whole. "I go for smart, protective, and loyal dogs," Wilson says, "and that's what I went for in my man too!"

3 If you have both a spouse and a dog right now, count all the things they have in common (though you shouldn't necessarily share this information with them). If you have one but not the other, let one's personality be a guide to what you would seek in the other.

4 We can't choose our family members, but we sure can pick our spouses and dogs. You love athletic types? Get a retriever. Life of the party makes you swoon? The Jack Russell terrier is your dog. You want athletic and serious? Try a bloodhound.

5 We have an internal checklist in the selection of a companion: Are our play levels well matched? Is she demanding? Protective? How much does he shed? And best of all – is this one trainable?! But those checklists are different for everyone. "What makes one person feel complete drives another up the wall," Wilson points out.

Retriever

Jack Russell terrier

Bloodhound

German shepherd

Afghan hound

Chow

6 Just ask our mothers, our friends, our dog trainers – we don't always choose wisely. Some people are just always getting their fingers bitten. And even when we do find the right one, there are drawbacks. Lots of women, Wilson adds, choose a dog that will make them feel safe. Wilson says she herself is like this. Her husband and her dogs (German shepherds and Australian shepherds) are very brave and protective of her. "I pay a price for that preference, though," she says, laughing, "with occasional bouts of serious barking."

7 As in any romance, appearance counts in the chemistry of love. Ah! The glamor of an Afghan hound, the piercing blue eyes of a Siberian husky. But in love, there is just no accounting for taste. Whether a friend is showing us her new boyfriend or a Boston terrier, we have often thought, "What on earth does she see in him?" "Through the eyes of love," Wilson says, "anything is beautiful." And we cannot see the flaws that others do in our spouses or our dogs.

8 Ultimately with any kind of love, it's what's under the skin that lasts. "If you're attracted just by the physical alone," Wilson says, "it can be a disaster. Like a mail-order bride, that gorgeous redheaded chow may be better in the picture than on your couch."

Adapted from *The Boston Globe*.

Before you read

Relating to the topic

Look at the pictures on the opposite page. Use the characteristics in the box below to describe each dog.

athletic	glamorous	playful	serious
brave	gorgeous	protective	smart

Reading

Scanning

Scan the text to find out how the writer describes each dog. Then read the whole text.

After you read

Recognizing audience

A **Who do you think the text was written for? Check (✔) the correct answer.**

____ 1. men

____ 2. women

____ 3. pet owners

Understanding main ideas

B **Write the number of each paragraph next to its main idea.**

_3_ a. People should choose dogs and spouses with similar characteristics.

____ b. Appearance alone should not be the basis for a good relationship.

____ c. People choose dogs and human companions based on appearance.

____ d. You can choose spouses and dogs with characteristics you admire.

____ e. People have very different tastes in dogs.

____ f. Our attitudes are revealed in the type of dogs and spouses we choose.

____ g. People look for qualities that they don't have when choosing dogs or spouses.

____ h. Sometimes people choose spouses or dogs with bad qualities.

Answer these questions.

Relating reading to personal experience

C

1. What characteristics are important to you in choosing a mate?
2. What characteristics are important to you in choosing a pet?
3. Do you agree with the writer's claim? Why or why not?

Love Song for Lucinda

Langston Hughes (1902-1967) *was one of the most important writers of the African American artistic movement in the 1920s. He is best known for his poetry. His novels, plays, essays, and children's books are insightful, colorful portrayals of black life in America.*

Love
Is a ripe plum
Growing on a purple tree.
Taste it once
And the spell of its enchantment
Will never let you be.

Love
Is a bright star
Glowing in far Southern skies.
Look too hard
And its burning flame
Will always hurt your eyes.

Love
Is a high mountain
Stark in a windy sky.
If you
Would never lose your breath
Do not climb too high.

Ashes of Life

Edna St. Vincent Millay (1892-1950) *One of the most popular poets of her era, Edna St. Vincent Millay was admired for using traditional verse forms to express simple, strong emotions. She was awarded the Pulitzer Prize for poetry in 1923.*

LOVE has gone and left me and the days are all alike;
  Eat I must, and sleep I will,—and would that night were here!
But ah!—to lie awake and hear the slow hours strike!
  Would that it were day again!—with twilight near!

Love has gone and left me and I don't know what to do;
  This or that or what you will is all the same to me;
But all the things that I begin I leave before I'm through,—
  There's little use in anything as far as I can see.

Love has gone and left me,—and the neighbors knock and borrow,
  And life goes on forever like the gnawing of a mouse,—
And to-morrow and to-morrow and to-morrow and to-morrow
  There's this little street and this little house.

Before you read

Predicting

The pictures below are related to the poems on the opposite page. Predict what each poem is about.

Love Song for Lucinda

Ashes of Life

Reading

Scanning

Scan the text to check your predictions. Then read the whole text.

After you read

Understanding main ideas

A **Check (✔) the ideas that are expressed in each poem.**

Love Song for Lucinda

✔ 1. Love is like a plum. Once you taste it, you will want more.
____ 2. Love is like a plum. Its sweetness doesn't last very long.
____ 3. Love is like a star. It is sometimes hard to find.
____ 4. Love is like a star. It can burn and hurt you.
____ 5. Love is like climbing a mountain. You can get hurt.
____ 6. Love is like climbing a mountain. You will never reach the top.

Ashes of Life

____ 1. Time passes quickly now that love has gone.
____ 2. Life is boring without love.
____ 3. Life seems pointless without love.
____ 4. Nowadays it's easy to get angry with people.
____ 5. There is no more excitement in life.
____ 6. Tomorrow will be better.

Rhyming

B **Fill in the blanks with rhyming words from the poems.**

Love Song for Lucinda	
1. tree	*be*
2. skies	________
3. sky	________

Ashes of Life			
4. alike	________	7. me	________
5. here	________	8. borrow	________
6. do	________	9. mouse	________

Relating reading to personal experience

C **Answer these questions.**

1. Which poem do you prefer? Why?
2. The first poet compares love to a plum, a star, and a mountain. What would you compare love to?
3. The second poet describes the feelings of someone after a relationship ends. What advice would you give someone who feels like this?

Vocabulary expansion

A Check (✔) the idioms that are new for you.

_____ *be crazy about*: like someone very much

_____ *be head over heels in love*: love someone very much

_____ *be in love at first sight*: fall in love with someone as soon as you see him or her

_____ *be madly in love*: have a very strong, romantic attraction for someone

_____ *be made for*: be perfectly suitable to be romantically involved with

_____ *be swept off (your) feet*: fall in love with someone almost as soon as you meet him or her

_____ *be the love of (one's) life*: be the person one loves more than anyone else

_____ *fall in love*: start to be in love with someone

_____ *have a crush on*: have a strong feeling of attraction or love that does not last very long

B Answer the questions.

1. Do you know anyone who is head over heels in love?
2. Do you have any friends that you think are made for each other?
3. Have you ever had a crush on someone?
4. What kinds of crazy things do people do when they first fall in love?
5. Do you believe in love at first sight?
6. Have you ever been swept off your feet?

C Think about characters in recent movies or TV programs you have seen. Which idioms in exercise A could describe these characters?

Love and you

Work in groups. Make a list of all the English love songs you know. Then decide which song is the best. Write down as many of the lyrics of the song as you can remember.

UNIT 12 Fear

You are going to read three texts about fear. First, answer the questions in the boxes.

READING 1

Flying? No fear

Read this newspaper article to learn some ways that people can learn to cope with their fear of flying.

1. Are you afraid of flying? If so, what causes you the greatest worry — takeoff, landing, unusual noises, or turbulence?
2. How do you think people should deal with their fear during a flight?

READING 2

Don't fight a good fright

Why do people enjoy fantasy frights, such as horror movies or haunted houses? This article tries to explain our love of fear.

1. Do you enjoy watching horror movies, going to haunted houses, or going on scary rides at an amusement park? Why or why not?
2. Do you think it is harmful to experience brief moments of intense fear? Why or why not?

READING 3

Fighting stage fright

Do professional performers ever suffer from stage fright? Read this newspaper article to find out what some of them say about the subject.

1. How do you think professional singers and musicians feel before a performance?
2. Do you think people can learn not to be frightened before a performance? If so, what strategies do you know about?

Vocabulary

Find out the meanings of the words in the box. Then circle the feelings that you have experienced.

anxiety	phobia	tearful	terrified
panic	scared to death	tension	uneasiness

Flying? No fear

1 A study claims that 20 percent of the population is scared of flying. Can a course help ease the dread that some people feel about flying?

2 I am sitting with my wife, who is afraid to fly, and another 120 strangers in a hotel near Heathrow airport. Psychologist Dr. Keith Stoll and 16 other experts are taking us through a one-day fear of flying course.

3 In the morning, our fears are addressed. Pilot Richard Parkinson gives a clear explanation of how an airplane flies, and talks about the parts that cause most anxiety. Turbulence, or sudden movements of the plane, is the biggest trigger. It's uncomfortable, but common, and Parkinson explains how planes are built to deal with it.

4 The afternoon is more psychological. Fear of flying, like many other phobias, is marked by "catastrophizing" – obsessively thinking about disasters. The simplest solution, says Stoll, involves mental discipline: Simply stop yourself. The moment you find yourself picturing the worst, think about something more pleasant. If you do it often enough, the habit will weaken.

5 At the back of everyone's minds is the 40-minute flight at the end of the day on a 757. The question is, who will get on the plane?

6 There are different levels of anxiety in the group. Some are simply nervous, others truly terrified. Georgina Chapman, 24, is somewhere in the middle. She has flown many times, but her fear has grown with each trip. It's a surprisingly common problem: People remember every moment of uneasiness during years of flying, while they forget the peaceful trips. As a result, they increasingly expect the worst.

7 "I went to Bali and spent two weeks lying on the beach," says Georgina. "It sounds like fun, but it wasn't. I spent the whole time looking up at the planes, terrified at the thought I'd have to get on one to get home."

8 This is the second course for 36-year-old David Green: The first time he couldn't leave the hotel for the airport. He's a big man, reluctant to show fear, but his hands are white. "I only want to go to Majorca for a holiday with my family, but right now I just can't," he says. "The worst thing is, I think I'm starting to communicate my fear to my son."

9 Towards the end of the afternoon, the tension is rising. The hour approaches. My wife is pale, but relatively calm. Some of the others never make it. A handful won't leave the hotel. David Green nervously walks to the plane, walks back, boards again.

10 The flight is strange. There are a lot of emotions: First-time fliers happily wonder why they'd been worried, experienced fliers with nervous smiles talk about the reduction in their anxiety and, here and there, a tearful passenger is having a terrible panic attack. Everyone is invited for their minute with the pilots. They make a point of informing passengers of the reason for every thump, clunk, and patch of turbulence.

11 When we land, most passengers are smiling. Georgina Chapman is happy: "It's definitely helped. I was much more comfortable." David Green stepped on and off the plane once too often – and stayed in the boarding area. "Next time," he says. "Next time I'll get on." I hope he does. He looks like a man who needs a vacation.

Adapted from *The Sunday Times*.

Before you read

Using previous knowledge

What happens during a fear of flying course? Check (✔) the statements you think are true.

____ 1. A pilot explains how an airplane flies.

____ 2. The participants watch a video of workers building an airplane.

____ 3. The participants meet people who have survived plane crashes.

____ 4. Speakers explain how airplanes deal with turbulence.

____ 5. A psychologist tells participants how to stop imagining disasters.

____ 6. The participants take a short flight.

____ 7. At the end of the course, the participants have a party on an airplane.

Reading

Scanning

Scan the text to check your answers. Then read the whole text.

After you read

Recognizing similarity in meaning

A **Match each word or phrase with a word or phrase that is similar in meaning.**

_b_	1. *scared* (par. 1)	a. *cause* (par. 3)
____	2. *trigger* (par. 3)	b. *afraid* (par. 2)
____	3. *pale* (par. 9)	c. *get on* (par. 5)
____	4. *a handful* (par. 9)	d. *some* (par. 9)
____	5. *board* (par. 9)	e. *white* (par. 8)

Understanding details

B **Complete each sentence with *All*, *None*, or *Some*.**

1. ___*All*___ of the course participants were adults.
2. ________ of them had taken a fear of flying course before.
3. ________ of them had flown before.
4. ________ of them got on a plane at the beginning of the course.
5. ________ of them took a short flight at the end of the course.
6. ________ of them succeeded in overcoming their fear of flying.

Relating reading to personal experience

C **Answer these questions.**

1. Would you recommend that someone with a fear of flying take this course? Why or why not?
2. Have you ever had a bad experience on a plane? If so, what happened?
3. Do you have any phobias, such as a fear of heights or elevators? If so, how do you deal with these fears?

Don't fight a good fright

1 Mark DeMatteis had just paid money to walk past creepy clowns, and a screaming madman with a chainsaw, and he was loving every minute of it. "I love to be scared. . . . I love the art of it," said the 38-year-old connoisseur of haunted houses and horror movies. He's never experienced a fantasy fright he didn't like.

2 There's no doubt that real life can be scary sometimes, or even dangerous to one's health. That is evidently part of the reason people love a good fright in a haunted house or movie theater, which they can manage with little actual risk involved.

3 "It's a gratifying thing for people to confront something that resembles something they're really scared of, and come out on the other side knowing, 'I did it, I controlled it, I didn't fall apart,' " said Glenn Sparks, a Purdue University professor who has studied how people handle fear from media images.

4 He said that in modern society, a young male's ability to withstand a scary image or amusement park thrill ride could be a rite of passage to prove himself.

5 Sparks has observed how haunted houses and horror films are common dating experiences for young couples. He believes that males and females have expectations of how the other should act. "If a male goes into one of those situations and expresses mastery and control, females tend to find him more attractive and he is admired more," he said. "Similarly, for a female, the normal reaction is to show fear. If a female doesn't show that, the female becomes less attractive." When asked who reacts the most in haunted houses, DeMatteis supported the theory. "Girls 16 to 30 are the main ones that scream, without a doubt."

6 It's rare for fright alone to actually harm anyone, although DeMatteis recalled working at a haunted house a few years ago where a man collapsed inside. Dr. Cyril Wecht, who admits that some movie scenes disturbed him as a young man, is unaware of any cases in which people reacted to frightening images so strongly that they were literally scared to death. However, he doesn't rule out the possibility. It depends on the strength of the person's heart at the time he experiences intense fear. Wecht and others say that a real-life fear is more likely to affect one's health than deliberate exposure to frightening settings.

7 Recently, Theresa Streshenkoff, 16, was on her third trip to the haunted house even though she said she's often scared. Her first time this year, the high school student ran screaming from a frightening figure in costume. She still felt a thrill going through again days later, even after she knew what to expect. "It isn't supposed to be fun to be scared, but if it's frightening and you know it's not going to hurt you, it's fun," she explained.

READING TIP

The adverb *literally* shows that the exact meaning of a word or phrase, not the idiomatic meaning, is intended. For example, the idiomatic meaning of *scared to death* is "very frightened." *Literally scared to death* means that someone was so scared that he or she died.

Adapted from *Pittsburgh Post-Gazette*.

Before you read

Predicting

Look at the headline and picture on the opposite page. Then check (✔) the statement that you think best describes what the text is about.

____ 1. People should confront things that frighten them so that they can learn to control their fear.

____ 2. People should avoid things that frighten them so that they don't get hurt.

____ 3. People can enjoy being frightened when they know nothing bad will happen.

Reading

Skimming

Skim the text to check your prediction. Then read the whole text.

After you read

Guessing meaning from context

A Find the words in *italics* in the reading. Circle the meaning of each word.

1. When you *withstand* something frightening, you **face** / **talk about** / **show** your fear. (par. 4)
2. In a *rite of passage*, young people do certain actions to show they have become **young adults** / **good children** / **smart students.** (par. 4)
3. In this situation, when a young male wants to *prove himself,* he wants to show that he is **brave** / **intelligent** / **popular.** (par. 4)
4. When you *rule out* something, you decide that it is **impossible** / **scary** / **true.** (par. 6)

Understanding details

B Mark each sentence true (*T*), false (*F*), or does not give the information (*?*).

__?__ 1. Horror movies are getting scarier and scarier.

____ 2. Horror movies and scary things at amusement parks are often dangerous for people who get scared easily.

____ 3. People who are not frightened at horror movies or amusement parks also don't get scared easily in real life.

____ 4. Young males like to show they are "men" by not showing fear.

____ 5. Professor Sparks believes that females like males who don't show their fear.

____ 6. Professor Sparks believes that males like females who don't show their fear.

Relating reading to personal experience

C Answer these questions.

1. What is the last scary movie you saw? Which parts were the most frightening? How did you react during the scary parts?
2. Do you agree that it's fun to do scary things when you know they are not going to hurt you?
3. Do you agree that females find males who don't show fear more attractive? Do males find females who don't show fear less attractive? Why do you think some people have these ideas?

Fighting stage fright

1 Fall down as you come onstage. That's an odd trick. Not recommended. But it saved the pianist Vladimir Feltsman when he was a teenager back in Moscow. The veteran cellist Mstislav Rostropovich tripped him purposely to cure him of pre-performance panic, Mr. Feltsman said. "All my fright was gone. You already fell. What else could happen?"

2 Musicians use many different strategies against stage fright and its signs: icy fingers, shaky limbs, racing heart, blank mind. Teachers and psychologists offer strategies too. In recent years, schools have started addressing anxiety in courses dealing with performance techniques or career preparation.

3 Teachers and therapists offer wide-ranging advice, from basics like learning pieces inside out to mental disciplines: visualizing a performance, for instance, and taking steps to relax. Don't deny that you're jittery, they urge; some excitement is natural, even necessary for dynamic playing. And play publicly often, simply for the experience.

4 Diane Nichols, a psychotherapist, suggests steps for the moments before performance, "Take two deep abdominal breaths, open up your shoulders, then smile," she says. "And not one of these 'please don't kill me' smiles. Then choose three friendly faces in the audience, people you would communicate with and make music to, and make eye contact with them." She wants performers not to think of the audience as a judge.

5 Lynn Harrell suffered extreme stage fright some 30 years ago as the principal cellist in the Cleveland Orchestra. "There were times when I got so nervous I was sure the audience could see my chest responding to the throbbing. It was just total panic. I came to a point where I thought, 'If I have to go through this to play music, I think I'm going to look for another job.'" Recovery, he said, involved developing humility – recognizing that whatever his talent, he was fallible, and that an imperfect concert was not a disaster.

6 Extreme demands by mentors or parents are often at the root of stage fright, says Dorothy DeLay, a well-known violin teacher. She tells young teachers under her wing to demand only what their students can always achieve.

7 It is not only young artists who suffer, of course. The legendary pianist Vladimir Horowitz's nerves were famous. "The great tenor Franco Corelli, they had to push him on stage," soprano Renata Scotto recalled.

8 Actually, success can make things worse. "In the beginning of your career, when you're scared to death, nobody knows who you are, and they don't have any expectations," soprano June Anderson said. "There's less to lose. Later on, when you're known, people are coming to see you, and they have certain expectations. You have a lot to lose."

9 "I never stop being nervous until I've sung my last note," said Ms. Anderson.

Adapted from *The New York Times*.

Before you read

Predicting

Look at the picture on the opposite page and the words and phrases below. Then check (✔) those you think you will read in the text.

____ 1. *fall down*	____ 5. *icy fingers*	____ 9. *screaming*
____ 2. *onstage*	____ 6. *shaky limbs*	____ 10. *jittery*
____ 3. *laughter*	____ 7. *racing heart*	____ 11. *applause*
____ 4. *panic*	____ 8. *blank mind*	____ 12. *throbbing*

Reading

Scanning

Scan the text to check your predictions. Then read the whole text.

After you read

Guessing meaning from context

A Find the words in *italics* in the reading. Then complete the sentences.

tripped (par. 1)
learning pieces inside out (par. 3)
visualizing a performance (par. 3)
fallible (par. 5)
mentors (par. 6)
under her wing (par. 6)

1. It's important to practice music until you play it perfectly. Learning pieces inside out can be very useful.
2. ______________ teach you and give you a lot of valuable career advice.
3. We are all ______________. Everybody makes mistakes.
4. I was walking when he put his leg in front of me. After I ______________ and fell, he apologized.
5. She really became responsible for him when she took him ______________.
6. Imagine yourself playing the piano before an audience. ______________ will allow you to feel less nervous.

Understanding text organization

B Number the information about stage fright in the order it is mentioned, from 1 (first) to 6 (last).

____ a. people with stage fright
__1__ b. an experience with stage fright
____ c. its symptoms
____ d. possible cures
____ e. its causes
____ f. the effects of success

Relating reading to personal experience

C Answer these questions.

1. Have you ever spoken or performed in front of an audience? If so, was it a good experience? Why or why not?
2. Have you ever suffered from stage fright? If so, what were your symptoms?
3. Which piece of advice in the text do you think is the most helpful? Why?

Vocabulary expansion

A **Answer the questions with the words in the box.**

afraid	frighten	frightening	scared	scary	terrified
anxiety	frightened	panic	scared to death	tension	

1. When people experience a little fear, how do they feel?
   They feel ____________ , ____________ , or ____________ .
2. When people experience extreme fear, how do they feel?
   They feel ____________ or ____________ .
3. What things make people fearful?
   ____________ and ____________ things make them fearful.
4. What other emotions do people sometimes feel when they're fearful?
   They sometimes feel ____________ , ____________ , or ____________ .
5. Why do people feel fearful?
   Things ____________ them.

B **Here are some other words and expressions related to fear. Write a word or expression from exercise A that is similar in meaning. (Note: In some cases, more than one word is correct.)**

1. After the bad flight to Miami, I was *fearful* of getting on a plane again. *scared*
2. He had many *hair-raising* experiences when he first learned to fly. ____________
3. I was *scared out of my wits* the first time I got on a plane; I almost didn't get on the plane. ____________
4. I was so *petrified* when I heard the loud noise that I couldn't move. ____________
5. Flying doesn't *scare* me. ____________
6. The pilot *gave* me *a fright* when he said we had to return to the airport. ____________
7. Flying in a small plane can be a *terrifying* experience for people who are afraid to fly. ____________

Fear and you

Work in groups. Describe a very frightening experience you have had. Answer these questions.

1. Where were you?
2. How long ago did this happen?
3. What exactly happened?

UNIT 13 The paranormal

You are going to read three texts about the paranormal. First, answer the questions in the boxes.

READING 1

Using hypnosis to combat stress

Do you ever feel stressed? Read this newspaper article about an unusual program to help students relieve their stress.

1. Do you suffer from stress before an exam? How does stress affect your test results?
2. Do you think hypnosis is a good idea for students who suffer from stress before tests? Why or why not?

READING 2

Psychic solves crimes

This newspaper article reveals how a psychic can help the police solve crimes.

1. What is a psychic? How do you think a psychic could help the police find criminals?
2. Do you think countries with serious crime problems should use psychics to help the police? Why or why not?

READING 3

What is a near-death experience (NDE)?

People say that something unusual happens to those who come close to dying. Read this website to find out what that "something" might be.

1. What have you heard about people who had strange experiences when they were near death?
2. Do you believe that people can have out-of-body experiences, that is, leave their bodies? Why or why not?

Vocabulary

Find out the meanings of the words in the box. Then match each with the title of the text in which you think they will appear.

altered state of mind	meditation	unidentified beings
bliss	sacred beings	visions

1. Using hypnosis to combat stress ______________
2. Psychic solves crimes ______________
3. What is a near-death experience (NDE)? ______________

Using hypnosis to combat stress

1 Some schools in Britain are offering hypnosis to students as young as 10 years old in an effort to help improve their test results.

2 The plan will start in more than 200 schools in West Yorkshire.[1] If successful, schools across Britain could adopt hypnosis for those who want the help. They are targeting students who suffer from stress and nerves. All the students who undergo hypnosis will be volunteers, and parents will have to give permission. As part of the program, the students will also learn breathing exercises and meditation to help them relax.

3 Trained hypnotists will be available to put the youngsters in "an altered state of mind" as they study for their examinations.

4 Dr. Phil Jones, an educational psychologist and trained hypnotist, told the *Straits Times*: "Members of the public often get a wrong impression about hypnosis from stage performers." Used by qualified psychologists, it is very safe and has a proven record of effectiveness. "We want to help children who get so nervous that their studies and exam performances suffer."

5 Dr. Paul Richardson, a member of the Society of Hypnotherapists, told the *Straits Times*: "This is a very good idea. It is not uncommon for many children to be nervous in the time leading up to tests – and hypnosis should be of great benefit to them. If carried out by trained people, hypnosis can be of great help to people who are nervous and need calming, and those suffering from stress."

6 This unusual way of trying to relieve school-time stress comes after many educators have criticized the examination system in Britain. They say there is non-stop testing of youngsters, from the age of five to the time they finish secondary school – causing constant nervousness among many students.

7 The strain of lessons will only increase. When they reach secondary schools, students who fall behind in English and math will be offered extra lessons during lunch breaks, after school, and on weekends.

8 Although some educators agree that stress is a widespread problem among students, they have doubts about the use of hypnosis to alleviate it.

9 Mr. Gerald Hawker, head of one of the schools in the West Yorkshire region said: "Who knows what effect playing with minds will have on young, vulnerable children?"

10 Teaching union representative Nigel de Gruchy said: "I am sorry education has come to this. Will we end up using drugs to enhance performance?"

1 a region in northwest England

Adapted from *The Straits Times*.

Before you read

Predicting

Check (✔) the information you think you will read about in the text.

_____ 1. the reasons why schools use hypnosis

_____ 2. the kinds of students who try hypnosis

_____ 3. the techniques used to hypnotize students

_____ 4. the results of hypnosis with students in different countries

_____ 5. the financial cost of using hypnosis in schools

Reading

Scanning

Scan the text to check your predictions. Then read the whole text.

After you read

Guessing meaning from context

A Find the words in *italics* in the reading. Then match each word with its meaning. (Be careful! There is one extra answer.)

__d__	1. *volunteers* (par. 2)	a. happening in many places
_____	2. *effectiveness* (par. 4)	b. improve
_____	3. *carried out* (par. 5)	c. having the intended results
_____	4. *widespread* (par. 8)	d. people who do something without being forced or paid
_____	5. *vulnerable* (par. 9)	e. done
_____	6. *enhance* (par. 10)	f. easily harmed
		g. students who have to take tests

Understanding details

B Mark each sentence true (*T*) or false (*F*).

__T__ 1. Not all students need hypnosis.

_____ 2. Teachers will decide who should get hypnosis.

_____ 3. If students do not want to undergo hypnosis, they can do breathing exercises and meditation instead.

_____ 4. Some education professionals believe that too much testing causes stress in students.

_____ 5. Some people worry that hypnosis could have a bad effect on children.

Relating reading to personal experience

C Answer these questions.

1. How do you relax before taking a test?
2. Do you think hypnosis can help people? If so, in what ways?
3. What other problems do you think hypnosis can help?

volunteer
altered
4 effective
stress is a widespread problem
enhance

Psychic solves crimes

1 A psychic who secretly helped Scotland Yard[1] solve hundreds of crimes over more than 20 years spoke about her extraordinary relationship with the police. Nella Jones, 64, revealed details about a series of cases where her information led directly to the criminals. The Metropolitan Police, who had never publicly acknowledged her role, held a dinner in her honor to express gratitude for her "invaluable" help in catching a range of criminals.

2 Her relationship with the police began in 1974, shortly after the theft of Johannes Vermeer's painting *The Guitar Player* from Kenwood House,[2] London. Ms. Jones soon began to receive visions, or "psychic clues," that told her the painting was in a cemetery in east London. The police found it, undamaged and wrapped in newspaper, in St. Bartholomew's churchyard in the city. "After that, word got round, and it was not long before other police officers came to call, asking if I could help out," she said.

3 Since then, she has helped solve various murders, forecasted where bombs would be placed, and traced money stolen in bank robberies. "The sensations you feel are sometimes awful," she said. "You often pick up the pain of the victims. I sometimes think it's not a gift, but a curse." In 1989, Ms. Jones almost single-handedly solved a murder in southeast London. Investigating officers took her to the room where someone had killed an old woman. She immediately ran out into the street, telling officers she could see the letters EARL and a red Cortina[3] with a rusty roof rack. On a nearby road was Earl Motors. Investigations by police revealed that a man had recently sold the garage owners a red Cortina with a rusty roof rack. He turned out to be the murderer.

4 "Nella has given invaluable assistance on a number of murders," said Detective Chief Inspector Arnie Cooke, "We have to keep an open mind to the paranormal. It would be stupid not to follow up the leads she gives us. There are a lot of strange things happening."

5 Ms. Jones says everyone is born with abilities similar to hers, but few try to use them. "It's the most natural thing in the world."

6 Last year, the American government spent more than 18 million dollars on psychics to help fight terrorism. Ms. Jones, however, believes her days of helping the police — for which she never received any money — are nearly over. "I'm getting too old," she said. "I have seen and felt some terrible things. I don't even want to think about them now. Sometimes I think I've done my bit for society."

1 the central police headquarters of the United Kingdom
2 a museum
3 a kind of car

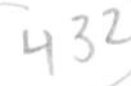

Adapted from *Sunday Telegraph.*

Before you read

Predicting

Look at the title and picture on the opposite page and the words below. Then check (✔) the words you think you will read in the text.

____	1. *police*	____	5. *television*	____	9. *robberies*
____	2. *theft*	____	6. *murders*	____	10. *victims*
____	3. *clues*	____	7. *bombs*	____	11. *investigations*
____	4. *cemetery*	____	8. *hospitals*	____	12. *terrorism*

Reading

Scanning

Scan the text to check your predictions. Then read the whole text.

After you read

Recognizing similarity in meaning

A **Find a word or phrase in the text that is similar in meaning to each word in *italics*.**

1. *helped* (par. 1) ______ *done my bit* ______ (par. 6, 3 words)
2. *information* (par. 1) ____________________ (par. 4)
3. *help* (par. 1) ____________________ (par. 4)
4. *cemetery* (par. 2) ____________________ (par. 2)
5. *various* (par. 3) ____________________ (par. 4, 3 words)
6. *feel* (par. 3) ____________________ (par. 3, 2 words)

Understanding details

B **Find and correct the four mistakes in each police report. (Note: The first mistake has been corrected.)**

1. Ms. Jones came to help us ~~before~~ *after* the theft of *The Guitar Player,* painted by Johannes Vermeer. She began to have visions about the painting. She saw that it was in Kenwood House. She went to look for it and found it. The story about the painting was in a newspaper.

2. The murder took place in southeast London. Someone had killed a young man. Ms. Jones lived near the room where the murder took place. She had a vision and saw a man named Earl. She also saw a red car. The police found out a man had recently bought a red car from a place called Earl Motors. The man was the murderer.

Relating reading to personal experience

C **Answer these questions.**

1. Do you agree that everyone is born with psychic abilities, but few try to use them? Do you think these powers are a gift or a curse?
2. Do you think you have psychic powers? If so, what visions have you had? If not, would you want to have this ability?
3. In what other ways could someone's psychic powers be useful to society?

What is a near-death experience (NDE)?

1 Most people who have come close to death say they remember nothing. However, a third or more may later report that "something happened." That "something" might be a near-death experience, or NDE. The near-death experience is among the most powerful experiences that a person can have. It may permanently change a person's perceptions of what is real and important.

2 One extraordinary aspect of NDEs is that a person's culture, religion, race, or education does not affect the pattern of the experience. The way people describe the NDE, however, varies according to their background and vocabulary.

3 There is no evidence that the type of experience is related to whether the person is religious or not, or has lived a "good" or "bad" life according to his or her society's standards. Nonetheless, an NDE often strongly affects how people continue to live their lives.

4 Most NDEs are pleasant, but others can be very frightening. For most people, the experience is joyful beyond words, although others tell of unpleasant or terrifying experiences. When understood, every type of NDE reveals things of deep meaning to the individual and to humankind in general.

5 No two NDEs are the same, but there is a pattern of experiences. Each experience includes one or more of these things:

- Feeling that the "self" has left the body and is overhead. The person may later be able to describe who was where and what happened, sometimes in detail.
- Moving through a dark space or tunnel
- Experiencing very powerful emotions, ranging from bliss to terror
- Encountering a light. It is usually golden or white, and said to be magnetic and loving; occasionally it is perceived negatively.
- Receiving a message such as, "It is not yet your time."
- Meeting others: maybe dead loved ones, recognized from life or not; sacred beings; unidentified beings and/or "beings of light"; sometimes symbols from one's own or other religious traditions
- Seeing and re-experiencing major or unimportant events in one's life
- Having a sense of understanding everything and knowing how the universe works
- Reaching a boundary — a cliff, fence, water, or some kind of barrier that one may not cross and still be able to return to life
- In some cases, entering a city or library
- Rarely, receiving previously unknown information about one's life (i.e., adoption or hidden parentage)
- Deciding to return, either voluntarily or involuntarily. If the return is voluntary, it is usually connected to unfinished responsibilities.
- Returning to the body

Adapted from *www.iands.org/nde.html.*

READING TIP The abbreviation *i.e.* means "that is." This abbreviation is used especially in writing to introduce specific information or to give examples after a general statement.

Before you read

Thinking about personal experience

Imagine having the experiences listed below. Then mark them pleasant (*P*), unpleasant (*U*), terrifying (*T*), or neutral (*N*).

_____ 1. feeling that you have left your body

_____ 2. moving through a dark space or tunnel

_____ 3. meeting dead loved ones

_____ 4. meeting sacred beings

_____ 5. understanding everything

_____ 6. re-experiencing events in your life

Reading

Skimming

Skim the text and check (✔) the best definition of a "near-death experience." Then read the whole text.

_____ 1. a frightening experience that happens to people who come close to death

_____ 2. thirteen things that happen to people who come close to death

_____ 3. common things that happen to people who come close to death

After you read

Guessing meaning from context

A Find the words in *italics* in the reading. Then write the correct word for each definition.

perception (par. 1) *background* (par. 2) *voluntary* (par. 5)
pattern (par. 2) *joyful* (par. 4)

background 1. the things that have made you into the person you are, especially family, experience, and education

_____ 2. having or causing great happiness

_____ 3. a recognizable way in which something happens

_____ 4. an awareness of things through the physical senses

_____ 5. done freely, by choice rather than by force

Understanding details

B Answer the questions.

1. Which near-death experiences involve physical movement?
2. Which near-death experiences involve visions?

Relating reading to personal experience

C Answer these questions.

1. Have you ever dreamed about a loved one who has died? If so, what do you remember about the dream?
2. Do you believe that people who come close to dying have similar experiences? Why or why not?
3. Have you ever had an experience that changed your life? If so, what happened?

Vocabulary expansion

Skim the dictionary entries. Then find the correct definition for each word in *italics* in the sentences below.

1. **case** /keis/ *n* [C] a particular situation or example of something • *It was a case of not knowing what to say.*
2. **case** /keis/ *n* [C] a matter that is a problem to be solved • *There were many reported cases of child abuse.*
3. **case** /keis/ *n* [C] arguments, facts, and reasons in support of or against something • *He presented the case against cutting the military budget.*

4. **catch** /kæʃ, ketʃ/ *v* [I/T] to get hold of a moving object or someone to prevent it from getting away • *She tossed him the car keys and yelled, "catch!"*
5. **catch** /kæʃ, ketʃ/ *v* [T] to see or hear (something), or to understand • *I'm sorry, I didn't catch what you said.*
6. **catch** /kæʃ, ketʃ/ *v* [T] to travel on (a train, bus, aircraft, etc.) • *He always catches the 6:05 train out of Grand Central station.*
7. **catch** /kæʃ, ketʃ/ *v* [T] to get (an illness) • *I don't want to catch a cold.*
8. **catch** /kæʃ, ketʃ/ *n* [C] a hidden problem or disadvantage • *That sales price sounds too good to be true — there must be a catch.*

9. **lead** /liːd/ *n* [C] information that allows a solution to be found • *The leads the detectives were following led to several arrests.*
10. **lead** /liːd/ *v* [I/T] to prepare the way for (something) to happen; cause • *Ten years of scientific research will lead to the development of a new drug.*
11. **lead** /liːd/ *v* [I/T] (esp. in sports or other competitions) to be in front, be first, or be winning • *After thirty minutes, the challengers are leading by two goals.*
12. **lead** /liːd/ *v* [T] to live (a particular type of life) • *She retired to Florida and still leads a busy life.*

13. **sense** /sens/ *n* the ability to make reasonable judgments • *If the boy had any sense he would be scared.*
14. **sense** /sens/ *n* [C] any of the five physical abilities to see, hear, smell, taste, and feel • *Women have a better sense of smell than men.*
15. **sense** /sens/ *n* [C] an awareness of something, or an ability to do or understand something • *I have a very bad sense of direction.*
16. **sense** /sens/ *n* [C] a meaning of a word or phrase • *This isn't a travel book in the usual sense of the word.*

__2__ a. The psychic was able to solve many *cases*.

____ b. The psychic made a good *case* for getting the police to go to the park.

____ c. At first the detective didn't *catch* what the psychic was saying.

____ d. The police didn't *catch* the criminal until he committed another crime.

____ e. The police are looking for some *leads* to find the murderer.

____ f. The psychic *leads* a quiet life now that she has retired.

____ g. Solving this crime will *lead* to the solution of other crimes.

____ h. The psychic had a *sense* that something bad was going to happen.

____ i. The police should have better *sense* than to believe a psychic.

The paranormal and you

Work in small groups. Do a survey of people's beliefs in the paranormal. First, come up with five questions about the topics below (or your own topics). Then ask five classmates, friends, or family members. Report your findings to the class.

astrology	fortune-telling	UFOs
ESP	ghosts	

Example: Do you believe in ghosts?

UNIT 14 Languages

You are going to read three texts about languages. First, answer the questions in the boxes.

READING 1

The day a language died

Read about the last speaker of a native American language and what the death of a language means for humanity.

1. What do you think are the most widely spoken languages in the world?
2. Do you know of any languages that have died out? If so, how do you feel about this?

READING 2

Aping language

This magazine article explains what we can learn about ourselves by trying to teach language to chimpanzees.

1. How do animals communicate?
2. Do you think animals can understand human language? How do you know?

READING 3

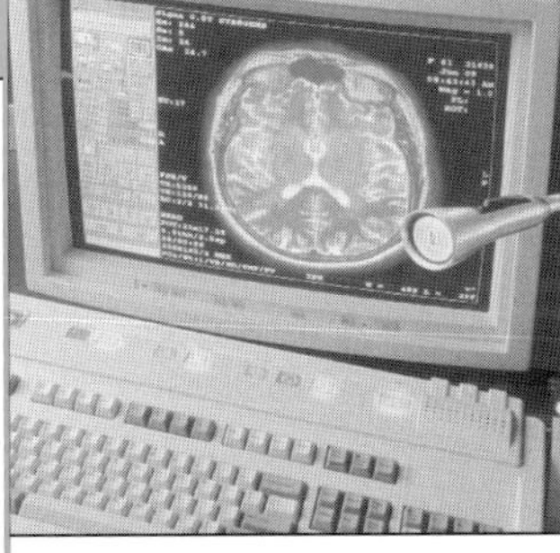

The bilingual brain

Why is learning a second language easier for children than it is for adults? Read about the parts of the brain and their roles in language learning at different ages.

1. What is the best age to start learning another language? Why?
2. Why is it easier for some people to learn a new language than it is for others?

Vocabulary

Find out the meanings of the words in *italics*. Then check (✔) the statements that are true about you.

_____ 1. Some *aspects* of reading are more difficult for me than others.

_____ 2. It is difficult for me to *convey* what I mean in another language.

_____ 3. My *native tongue* is easy for most people to learn.

_____ 4. I can speak more than one language *fluently*.

_____ 5. I have a good understanding of English *syntax*.

The day a language died

1 Recently another language died. Carlos Westez, more commonly known as Red Thunder Cloud, the last speaker of the Native American language Catawba, died at the age of 76. With his death, the Catawba language died too.

2 Anyone who wants to hear the songs of the Catawba can contact the Smithsonian Institution in Washington, D.C., where, back in the 1940s, Red Thunder Cloud recorded a series of songs for future generations. Some people might even try to learn some of these songs by heart. But Catawba is gone forever.

3 We are all aware of the damage that modern industry can cause the world's ecology, but few people are aware of the impact widely spoken languages have on other languages and ways of life. English has spread all over the world. Chinese, Spanish, Russian, and Hindi have become powerful languages as well. As these languages become more powerful, their use as tools of business and culture increases. As this happens, hundreds of languages that are spoken by a few die out all over the world.

4 Scholars believe there are around 6,000 languages around the world, but more than half of them could die out within the next 100 years. Aore is the language native to Vanuatu, located in the Pacific Ocean. Like Catawba before Red Thunder Cloud's death, it is spoken by that island's only remaining native inhabitant; so it, too, will soon die. A large number of Ethiopian languages are used by tiny numbers of people. Two speakers of the Ethiopian language Gafat were fine until a researcher took them out of their native jungle, at which point they caught cold and died. In New Guinea, more than 100 languages could disappear. In the Americas, 100 languages, each of which has fewer than 300 speakers, are dying out. North America, which once had hundreds of languages, has only about 100 languages left.

5 It was for this reason that Red Thunder Cloud's death made the news. He was one of the first to recognize the danger of language death and to try to do something about it. He was not actually born into the Catawba tribe, and the language was not his mother tongue. However, he was a frequent visitor to the Catawba reservation in South Carolina, where he learned the language. The songs he sang for the Smithsonian Institution helped to make Native American music popular. Now he is gone and the language is dead. What does it mean for the rest of us when a language disappears?

6 When a plant, insect, or animal species dies, it is easy to understand what has been lost. However, language is only a product of the mind. To be the last remaining speaker of a language must be a peculiarly lonely destiny, almost as strange and terrible as being the last surviving member of a dying species. When a language dies, we lose the possibility of a unique way of seeing and describing the world.

Adapted from *The Independent.*

Before you read

Using previous knowledge

How much do you know about languages? Answer these questions.

1. What languages have died? ____________________
2. What languages are in danger of dying? ____________________
3. How many languages are spoken in the world? ____________________
4. What languages are most widely spoken? ____________________

Reading

Scanning

Scan the text to check your answers. Then read the whole text.

After you read

Summarizing

A **Check (✔) the best summary of the text.**

____ 1. The death of Red Thunder Cloud marks the end of the Catawba language.

____ 2. Languages die when the last speakers of the language die.

____ 3. The disappearance of languages is a loss for the whole world.

____ 4. Some languages disappear because other languages are more widely spoken.

Restating and making inferences

B **Mark each sentence inference (*I*), restatement (*R*), or not in the text (*?*).**

1. Red Thunder Cloud . . .

__*R*__ a. spoke the Catawba language, but was not Catawba.

____ b. liked Native American music.

____ c. was concerned that the Catawba language could die.

____ d. earned a living by singing Catawba songs.

2. Some languages disappear because . . .

____ a. governments don't take responsibility for keeping them alive.

____ b. they are spoken by very few people.

____ c. they do not have a written form.

____ d. other languages are becoming more powerful.

3. In the future, . . .

____ a. some languages will continue to be powerful.

____ b. languages that are powerful today won't be powerful.

____ c. thousands of languages will disappear.

____ d. languages spoken by only hundreds of people will likely disappear.

Relating reading to personal experience

C **Answer these questions.**

1. What are some ways in which your native language is unique?
2. How would the world be different if everyone spoke the same language?
3. What can be done to help preserve rare languages?

Aping language

1 These are among the things Kanzi, a bonobo chimp, can do. When he hears "give the dog a shot," he grabs a syringe from objects on the floor, pulls off the cap and injects his stuffed dog. He understands the difference between "take the potato outdoors" and "go outdoors and get the potato," and between "put the water in the raisins" and "put the raisins in the water." Kanzi, now 17, also combines words (actually, shapes called lexigrams on a keyboard) in the correct order to produce "grab Matata," meaning that the chimp Matata was grabbed, and "Matata bite" meaning that Matata did the biting.

2 Impressive, yes. But does that mean Kanzi can use true language? Using language distinguishes humans from other animals. Using language requires syntax, or the use of word order to communicate meaning, as in the raisins-and-water phrases. Sue Savage-Rumbaugh, who directs the research on Kanzi and other chimps, believes that apes are capable of grammar as complex as [that] used by human 2-year-olds. But to others, apes fall short. If combinations like "Lana tomorrow scare snake river monster" are language, then 2-year-olds are Shakespeare.

3 It's been a long disagreement, but scientists recently announced results from studies that may resolve the argument. These studies looked at apes' brains for patterns of activity that produce language in humans. At Mount Sinai School of Medicine, researcher Patrick Gannon and his colleagues examined the brains of chimps that died natural deaths in zoos or labs. The team was looking for an area similar to one that the human brain uses to understand and produce language. This area, called the planum temporale (PT), receives sounds and attaches meaning to them. In 17 of 18 chimps, the PT was larger on the left side of the brain than the right. That is also the pattern in most people.

4 If research proves that chimps are communicating with the same parts of the brain humans use for language, it will be hard to argue that chimps do not have a language. Interestingly 99 percent of the genes between chimps and humans is identical.

If chimps use language structures, it suggests that our last common ancestor used these structures too. In that case, early humans might have had basic language. For now, the possibility is very controversial. Still, in learning about chimps we may also learn more about ourselves.

Adapted from *Newsweek*.

Before you read

Predicting

Look at these sentences from the text. Then answer the questions below.

Give the dog a shot.
Take the potato outdoors.
Go outdoors and get the potato.
Put the water in the raisins.
Put the raisins in the water.

1. Which sentences do you think Kanzi the chimp can understand?

   ____ a. all ____ b. some ____ c. none

2. Which sentences do you think Kanzi can produce with shapes on a keyboard?

   ____ a. all ____ b. some ____ c. none

Reading

Scanning

Scan the text to check your predictions. Then read the whole text.

After you read

Understanding main ideas

A **Write the number of the paragraph where the following information can be found.**

_4_ a. reasons the research into the brains of apes is important
____ b. findings of recent research into the brains of dead chimps
____ c. disagreement scientists have about whether chimps use true language
____ d. examples of findings from Savage-Rumbaugh's research

Understanding details

B **Answer these questions on a separate piece of paper.**

1. What is the disagreement between Savage-Rumbaugh and other scientists?
   Savage-Rumbaugh and other scientists disagree on whether or not apes are capable of using syntax.
2. What is the planum temporale (PT)?
3. How is the PT in chimps similar to the PT in humans?
4. What could the research into chimp brains tell us about early humans?

Relating reading to personal experience

C **Answer these questions.**

1. Do you think the kind of research discussed in the article is important? Why or why not?
2. Would you like to be able to communicate with animals? Why or why not?
3. If animals could talk to people, what do you think they would say? Why?

syntax

THE BILINGUAL BRAIN

1 When Karl Kim immigrated to the United States from Korea as a teenager ten years ago, he had a hard time learning English. Now he speaks it fluently, and recently had a unique opportunity to see how our brains adapt to a second language. Kim is a graduate student in the lab of Joy Hirsch, a neuroscientist in New York. He and Hirsch have recently found evidence that children and adults don't use the same parts of the brain when learning a second language.

2 The researchers used an instrument called an MRI (magnetic resonance imager) to study the brains of two groups of bilingual people. One group consisted of those who had learned a second language as children. The other consisted of people who, like Kim, learned their second language later in life. People from both groups were placed inside the MRI scanner. This allowed Kim and Hirsch to see which parts of the brain were getting more blood and were more active. They asked people from both groups to think about what they had done the day before, first in one language and then the other. They couldn't speak out loud, because any movement would disrupt the scanning.

3 Kim and Hirsch looked specifically at two language centers in the brain — Broca's area, believed to control speech production, and Wernicke's area, thought to process meaning. Kim and Hirsch found that both groups of people used the same part of Wernicke's area no matter what language they were speaking. But how they used Broca's area was different.

4 People who learned a second language as children used the same region in Broca's area for both languages. People who learned a second language later in life used a special part of Broca's area for their second language — near the one activated for their native tongue. How does Hirsch explain this difference? Hirsch believes that when language is first being programmed in young children their brains may mix all languages into the same area. But once that programming is complete, a different part of the brain must take over a new language.

5 A second possibility is simply that we may acquire languages differently as children than we do as adults. Hirsch thinks that mothers teach a baby to speak by using different methods such as touch, sound, and sight. And that's very different from sitting in a high school class.

READING TIP

Writers use acronyms because they are shorter and usually better known than the words they replace. Acronyms are created from the first letters of each word in a series of words. For example, *MRI* is an acronym for "magnetic resonance imager." The first time the acronym appears, it is often followed by parentheses with the words it replaces.

Adapted from *Discover.*

Before you read

Predicting

Look at the title on the opposite page. Then check (✔) the statement that you think will be the main idea of the text.

_____ 1. The article explains how people become bilingual.

_____ 2. The article describes the best ways to acquire languages at different ages.

_____ 3. The article describes research into the brains of bilingual people.

Reading

Skimming

Skim the text to check your prediction. Then read the whole text.

After you read

Restating

A **Compare the meaning of each pair of sentences. Write same (*S*) or different (*D*).**

_____ 1. When Karl Kim immigrated to the United States, he had a hard time learning English.
English was hard for Karl Kim to learn because he immigrated to the United States.

_____ 2. No matter what language they were speaking, both groups of people used the same part of Wernicke's area.
People who spoke the same language used the same part of Wernicke's area.

_____ 3. The brain may mix sounds and structures from all languages into the same area.
The same part of the brain might take in all the aspects of different languages.

Understanding details

B **Answer these questions on a separate piece of paper.**

1. What machine did the researchers use in their study?
   The researchers used an MRI.
2. What groups were studied?
3. What was the the subject of the study?
4. What were the people in the study asked to do?
5. What are the names of the areas of the brain that were studied?
6. What are the functions of the areas of the brain that were studied?
7. What were the findings of the study?

Relating reading to personal experience

C **Answer these questions.**

1. Is it important to know more than one language? Why or why not?
2. What do you think is the best way for teenagers and adults to learn a second language? Why?
3. If you could learn another language, which one would you choose? Why?

fluently

Vocabulary expansion

A **The prefix *bi-* means "two." The prefix *uni-* means "one." Match each word with its meaning.**

f	1. *bilingual*	a. involving two groups or countries
___	2. *unique*	b. involving only one group or country
___	3. *bilateral*	c. having more than one spouse at the same time
___	4. *unilateral*	d. bring together or combine
___	5. *bigamy*	e. being the only existing one of its type
___	6. *unify*	f. able to speak two languages

B **Look at the pictures. Then complete each word with *bi* or *uni*.**

1\.

uni form

2\.

___ cycle

3\.

___ cycle

4\.

___ noculars

5\.

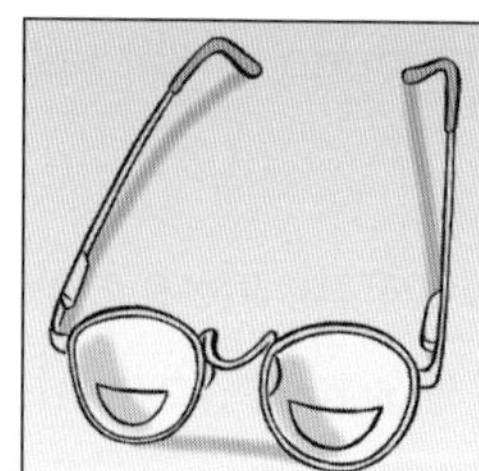

___ focals

6\.

___ weekly

Languages and you

Work in pairs. Make a list of DOs and DON'Ts people should follow to learn a foreign language. Then show others your list.

UNIT

15 The senses

You are going to read three texts about the senses. First, answer the questions in the boxes.

READING 1

Ice cream tester has sweet job

What is it like to have a job that requires tasting ice cream all day? Read this newspaper article about one lucky person.

1. How often do you eat ice cream? What is your favorite flavor?
2. What do you think taste-testers look for when they sample foods or beverages?

READING 2

Primer on smell

How much do you know about your sense of smell? This website answers some frequently asked questions about this sense.

1. Do you have a good, average, or poor sense of smell?
2. Do any smells remind you of certain people or places?

READING 3

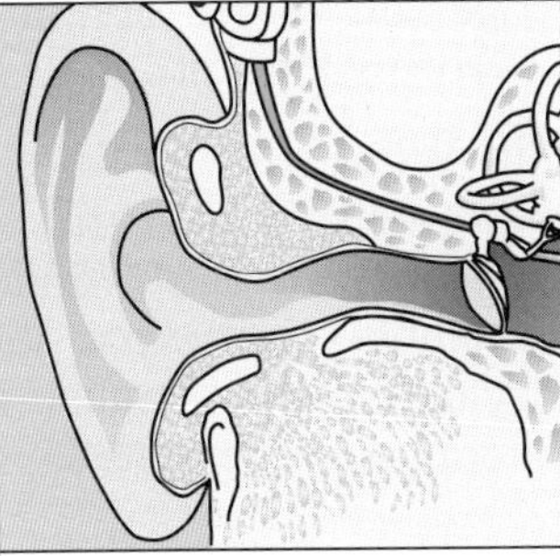

How deafness makes it easier to hear

How can deaf and hearing-impaired people create music? Read this newspaper article to learn some surprising information about hearing loss and musical ability.

1. Do you like the music of Beethoven? How do you think he was able to compose music after losing his hearing?
2. What aids do deaf people use to help them communicate?

Vocabulary

Find out the meanings of the words in the box. Then write each word under the correct heading.

accompaniment	harmony	odor	palate	taste buds
aroma	inner ear implant	olfactory	scent	texture

THE SENSE OF HEARING	THE SENSE OF SMELL	THE SENSE OF TASTE
______	______	______
______	______	______
______	______	______
______	______	______

Ice cream tester has sweet job

1 John Harrison has what must be the most wanted job in America. He's the official taster for Edys Grand Ice Cream, one of the nation's best-selling brands.

2 His taste buds are insured for $1 million. He gets to sample 60 ice creams a day at Edys headquarters in Oakland, California. And when he isn't doing that, he travels, buying Edys in supermarkets all over the country so that he can spot check for perfect appearance, texture, and flavor.

3 But the life of an ice cream taster, I realized after I met him last week, isn't all Cookies 'n' Cream – a flavor which Harrison invented, by the way. No, it's rigorous work, requiring discipline and selflessness.

4 For one thing, he doesn't swallow on the job. Like a coffee taster, Harrison spits. Using a gold spoon to avoid "off" flavors, he takes a smallish bite, swishes it around to introduce it to all 9,000 or so taste buds, smack-smack-smacks his lips to aerate the sample, and then gently inhales to bring the aroma up through the back of his nose. With each step, he's evaluating whether the ice cream conveys a harmonious balance of dairy, sweetness, and added ingredients – the three flavor components of ice cream.

5 Then, no matter how heavenly it is, he deposits it into a trash can. A full stomach makes for a dull palate.

6 During the workweek, other sacrifices must be made: no onions, garlic, or cayenne pepper; and no caffeine. Caffeine will block the taste buds, he says, so breakfast is a cup of herbal tea.

7 But it's all a small price to pay for what he calls the world's best job. His family has been in the ice cream business in one way or another for four generations, so Harrison has spent his entire life with it.

8 Yet, he has never lost his love for its cold, creamy sweetness. He even orders it in restaurants for dessert. On these occasions, he swallows, consuming about a quart weekly.

9 Americans eat 23.2 quarts per person of ice cream and other frozen dairy products annually.

10 What flavor does the best-trained ice-cream palate in America prefer? Vanilla, the best-selling variety. You should never call it plain vanilla. It's a very complex flavor, he says.

11 The night after we met, I had a plain salad for dinner and sadly thought about my future. I have to either do what Harrison does – learn to spit instead of swallow – or start interviewing more celery growers.

Adapted from *The Times-Picayune.*

Before you read

Predicting

The text is about an ice cream taste-tester. Check (✔) the questions you think the text will answer.

_____ 1. What ice cream company does he work for?

_____ 2. How much money does he earn?

_____ 3. How many kinds of ice cream does he taste on a typical day?

_____ 4. What is his favorite ice cream flavor?

_____ 5. What is the most popular ice cream flavor in the United States?

Reading

Scanning

Scan the text to check your predictions. Then read the whole text and answer the questions above.

After you read

Understanding details

A **Check (✔) the steps for tasting ice cream that are mentioned in the text.**

_____ 1.

_____ 2.

_____ 3.

_____ 4.

_____ 5.

_____ 6.

Making inferences

B **Answer the questions.**

1. Why are Harrison's taste buds insured for $1 million?
2. Why doesn't Harrison eat onions or garlic during the workweek?
3. Why does Harrison think he has "the world's best job"?
4. After her day with Harrison, why was the writer sad as she ate dinner?

Relating reading to personal experience

C **Answer these questions.**

1. Do you agree that Harrison has the best job in the world? What would your dream job be?
2. Would you be a good taste-tester? What kind of food would you like to test?
3. How would you describe the best meal you've ever eaten? The worst meal?

Primer on smell

In addition to bringing out the flavor of food, what does the sense of smell do for us?

1 Smell "gives us information about place, about where we are," says Randall Reed, a John Hopkins University professor whose specialty is the sense of smell. And smell tells us about people. "Whether we realize it or not, we collect a lot of information about who is around us based on smell," says Reed.

2 Even at a distance, odors can warn us of trouble — spoiled food, leaking gas, or fire. "It's a great alerter," offers Donald Leopold, a doctor at John Hopkins. "If someone lights a cigar three offices down, you know it right away."

3 With just a simple scent, smell can also evoke very intense emotion. Let's say, for example, that the smell is purple petunias, which have a rich spiciness no other petunia has, and that your mother died when you were three. You wouldn't need to identify the smell or to have conscious memories of your mother or her flower garden to feel sad if that sweet tang drifted up to the porch.

Compared with other mammals, how well do people detect smells?

4 That depends what you mean by "how well." We are low on receptors: Current estimates say that humans have roughly five million smell receptor cells, about as many as a mouse. A rat has some 10 million, a rabbit 20 million, and a bloodhound 100 million.

5 "Across species, there is a relatively good correlation between the number of receptor cells and olfactory acuity," says Reed. "You can hardly find the olfactory bulb in a human brain — it's a pea-sized object. In a mouse, it's a little bigger. It's bean-sized in a rat, about the size of your little finger in a rabbit, and the size of your thumb in a bloodhound."

Does that mean that our sense of smell is not very acute?

6 Not exactly. While we may not have the olfactory range of other creatures, the receptors we do have are as sensitive as those of any animal.

7 We can also think, making conscious (and successful) efforts to sort smells out. A trained "nose," such as that of a professional in the perfume business, can name and distinguish some 10,000 odors. Reed says that a perfume expert can sniff a modern scent that has a hundred different odorants in it, go into the lab, and list the ingredients. "In a modest amount of time, he comes back with what to you or me would smell like a perfect imitation of that perfume. It's amazing."

What happens to our sense of smell as we age?

8 Many people continue to have good olfactory function as they get older. That's not the rule, however. Leopold says that smell is generally highest in childhood, stays the same from the teens through the 50s, and drops starting at about 60 for women and 65 for men. "On average, your standard 80-year-old is only able to smell things half as well as your standard 20-year-old," says Leopold.

READING TIP

Dashes (—) are used to give examples. "Spoiled food, leaking gas, or fire" (par. 2) are examples of "trouble." Dashes are also used to give additional information. The words "it's a pea-sized object" (par. 5) give additional information about the olfactory bulb in a human brain.

Adapted from *www.jhu.edu/~jhumag/996web/smell.html.*

Before you read

Thinking about personal experience

How much do you know about your sense of smell? Answer these questions.

1. What does your sense of smell do?

____

2. Compared with other animals, how acute is your sense of smell?

____

3. What happens to your sense of smell as you age?

____

Reading

Scanning

Scan the text to check your answers. Then read the whole text.

After you read

Guessing meaning from context

A **Find the words in *italics* in the reading. Then match each word with its meaning. (Be careful! There are two extra answers.)**

d	1. *alerter* (par. 2)	a. a person with a good sense of smell
____	2. *evoke* (par. 3)	b. related to the ability to smell
____	3. *tang* (par. 3)	c. the typical situation
____	4. *drifted* (par. 3)	d. something that warns you of danger
____	5. *correlation* (par. 5)	e. a pleasantly strong smell
____	6. *olfactory* (par. 5)	f. connection
____	7. *sniff* (par. 7)	g. feel
____	8. *rule* (par. 8)	h. moved slowly
		i. cause
		j. smell

Understanding details

B **Which part of the text should the person who made each statement read? Write the correct heading.**

1. "My husband is a chef who can smell food and know exactly what is in it."
   Does that mean that our sense of smell is not very acute?
2. "I used to love the smell of roses, but their smell isn't as strong as it used to be."

   ____
3. "The smell of wood burning in a fireplace reminds me of the house where I grew up."

   ____

Relating reading to personal experience

C **Answer these questions.**

1. What is your favorite smell? What smells bother you?
2. What smells do you remember the most from your past?
3. What smells remind you of winter? What about spring, summer, and fall?

How deafness makes it easier to hear

1 Most people think of Beethoven's hearing loss as an obstacle to composing music. Yet it wasn't until the last decade of his life, when completely deaf, that Beethoven produced his most powerful works.

2 This is one of the most glorious cases of the triumph of will over adversity, but his biographer, Maynard Solomon, takes a different view. Beethoven's deafness certainly affected his personality. Solomon argues, however, that his deafness also "heightened his achievement as a composer . . . in his deaf world Beethoven could experiment free from the sounds of the outside world, free to create previously undreamed of forms and harmonies."

3 Hearing loss does not seem to affect the musical ability of musicians who become deaf. They continue to "hear" music with as much, or greater, accuracy than if they were actually hearing it being played.

4 Michael Eagar, who became deaf at the age of 21, describes this fascinating phenomenon. Within three months he found: "My former musical experiences began to play back to me . . . the sounds I 'heard' were not real but were indistinguishable from real hearing. Now, after more than 50 years, it is still rewarding to listen to these playbacks, to 'hear' music which is new to me and to find countless quiet accompaniments to all manners of my moods."

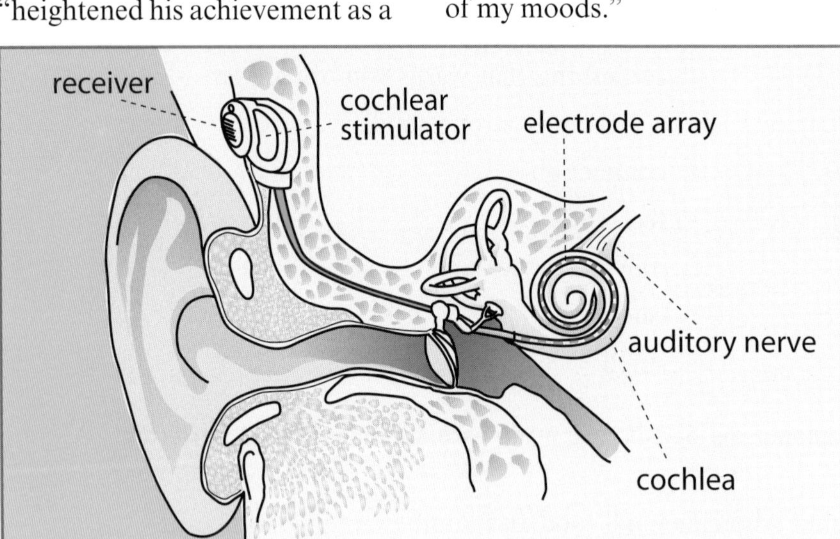

5 How is it that the world we see, touch, hear, and smell is both "out there" and at the same time *within* us? There is no better example of this connection between external stimulus and internal perception than the cochlear implant.[1] No man-made device could replace the ability to hear, but it might be possible to use the brain's remarkable power to make sense of the electrical signals it creates.

6 When Michael Eagar first "switched on" his cochlear implant, the sounds he heard were not at all clear. Gradually, with much hard work, he began to identify everyday sounds: "The bell of my old typewriter became clear almost at once, as did the insistent ringing of the telephone."

7 The primary purpose of the implant is to allow communication with others. When people spoke to him, he heard their voices "coming through like a long-distance telephone call on a poor connection." But when it came to his beloved music, the implant was of no help. So now when he wishes to appreciate music, he does as he always did. "I play the piano as before and hear it in my head at the same time. The movement of my fingers and the feel of the keys give added 'clarity' to hearing in my head."

8 Cochlear implants allow the deaf to hear again in a way that is not perfect, but which can change their lives. Still, as Michael Eagar discovered, when it comes to plugging in to musical harmonies, hearing is irrelevant. Even the most amazing cochlear implants would have been useless to Beethoven as he composed his Ninth Symphony at the end of his life.

1 A device, surgically placed in the ear, that changes sounds into electrical signals.

Adapted from *Sunday Telegraph*.

Before you read

Predicting

Look at the title on the opposite page. Then check (✔) the statement that you think will be the main idea of the text.

____ 1. The deaf don't hear external sounds, so they understand people's feelings better.

____ 2. Deaf musicians can learn to hear if they have an inner ear implant.

____ 3. Deaf musicians don't hear external sounds, so the music in their heads is clearer.

____ 4. Inner ear implants make it possible for the deaf to hear as well as other people.

Reading

Skimming

Skim the text to check your prediction. Then read the whole text.

After you read

Understanding reference words

A What do these words refer to?

1. *This* (par. 2, line 1) *that Beethoven could compose music when he was deaf*
2. *They* (par. 3, line 4) ____
3. *it* (par. 3, linc 7) ____
4. *it* (par. 5, line 13) ____
5. *their* (par. 8, line 4) ____

Understanding details

B Mark each sentence true (*T*), false (*F*), or does not give the information (*?*).

F 1. According to Solomon, Beethoven's deafness affected his personality more than it affected his ability to compose music.

____ 2. The cause of Beethoven's deafness is not known.

____ 3. Deaf musicians can "hear" music in their heads, but not the music that someone else is playing.

____ 4. Cochlear implants make it possible to hear everything better.

____ 5. With a cochlear implant, Beethoven could have composed more easily.

Relating reading to personal experience

C Answer these questions.

1. What do you think are some advantages of being able to hear? Some disadvantages?
2. Do you think deaf people should get cochlear implants? Why or why not? Why might a deaf person *not* want a cochlear implant?
3. What other successful people do you know of who are (or were) either blind or deaf?

Vocabulary expansion

Read the sentences. Then write the letter of the correct definition for the idioms in *italics*.

__e__ 1. Don't worry if you don't hear from me right away. I'll *touch base* a week or so after I arrive.

____ 2. I saw my friend's boyfriend at a party with another woman. I could *smell a rat.*

____ 3. It made Sue *see red* when the car didn't stop to let her cross the street.

____ 4. Dan knew very little about the subject he had to report on, but he got help and managed to *come up smelling like roses.*

____ 5. The accident was serious, and it's *touch-and-go* whether she'll be OK.

____ 6. Could you turn that music down? I can hardly *hear myself think.*

____ 7. The disagreement will *leave a bad taste in your mouth* if you don't find a solution.

____ 8. Mia and Tom want to buy different cars. They don't *see eye to eye*, so they haven't bought anything yet.

____ 9. I don't feel sorry for him. He has done the same thing to other people, so he just got *a taste of his own medicine.*

____ 10. If they win and we lose, we'll *never hear the end of it.*

a. achieve a better-than-expected result to a difficult, embarrassing, or unpleasant situation
b. realize that something dishonest is happening
c. cause you to have an unpleasant memory of something
d. uncertain
e. contact; communicate
f. continue to be told about something
g. become very angry
h. equally poor treatment
i. unable to pay attention to anything
j. agree

The senses and you

Work in groups. Choose a product that is normally advertised in a magazine or newspaper (for example, cars, food, or cosmetics), then create your own advertisement for it. In order to persuade people to buy your product, try to appeal to as many senses as possible. Show your ad to the other groups. Decide which ads appeal to the greatest number of senses.

UNIT

16 Heroes

You are going to read three texts about heroes. First, answer the questions in the boxes.

READING 1

What does it take to be a hero?

This magazine article examines the characteristics that are common to heroes and suggests that schools should do more to develop them.

1. How would you define a hero?
2. Who are some of your favorite heroes in history?

READING 2

Are athletes worthy heroes?

What is the difference between a sports star and a hero? This magazine article suggests some reasons why the two are not always the same.

1. Who are some of your favorite athletes?
2. Are athletes seen as heroes in your society? If so, why?

READING 3

The hero of my life

Read this excerpt from a book about someone who helped a stranger in a time of need and what it sometimes takes to be a personal hero.

1. What do some people do every day that makes them heroes?
2. When you have a problem, who do you go to for help? Is this person a hero to you?

Vocabulary

Find out the meanings of the words in *italics*. Then check (✔) the statements that you think are true.

_____ 1. Heroes are *competitive*.

_____ 2. Heroes are *courageous*.

_____ 3. Heroes are *noble*.

_____ 4. Heroes are *privileged*.

_____ 5. Heroes are *risk-takers*.

_____ 6. Heroes are *self-absorbed*.

_____ 7. Heroes are *selfless*.

_____ 8. Heroes are *thrill-seekers*.

What does it take to be a hero?

1 The world may seem not to have many heroes these days, but the number of potential heroes has never been greater. That's because every one of us — ourselves, our friends, even our kids — has heroic potential. There is plenty we can do to develop that untapped greatness and to ensure that the next generation gets the heroes it needs.

2 Though our personal heroes differ, we all share a common vision of what a hero is — and isn't. Temple University psychologist Frank Farley has created a list of six character traits he believes define the essence of heroism. Not every hero has them all, but the more one has, the better. If you seek greatness, either in yourself or your children, you should nurture these aspects of personality.

3 **Courage and strength** Whatever heroes are, they aren't cowards or quitters. Heroes maintain their composure — and even thrive — under adversity. Whether facing danger or enduring a long struggle or series of hardships, heroes never give up.

4 **Honesty** It's not a coincidence that in the United States, Presidents Abraham ("Honest Abe") Lincoln and George ("I cannot tell a lie") Washington are among the country's most beloved heroes. Deception violates the concept of heroism.

5 **Kindness, love, and generosity** Great people may fight fiercely for what they believe, but they are compassionate once the battle is over — toward friend and foe alike. A true hero demonstrates kindness to others.

6 **Skill, expertise, and intelligence** A hero's success comes from his or her talents and intelligence, rather than from chance. However, for the sake of modesty, heroes might well attribute their hard-earned achievements to luck.

7 **Risk-taking** "Even though many people won't take risks in their own life, they admire risk-taking in someone else," notes Farley, much of whose research has focused on Type-T personalities — people who are perpetual thrill-seekers. No matter what they do, heroes are willing to place themselves in some sort of danger.

8 **Objects of affection** We might be impressed on an intellectual level by somebody's accomplishments, but admiration is not enough. Heroes must win our hearts as well as our minds.

9 Farley warns, "Schools are not dealing enough with studying the lives of people who changed the world and did great things." A recent survey found that nearly half of kids have no heroes at all. This has serious implications. How can our children hope to rise above adversity — such as poverty or racism — without the example of the great men and women who came before them?

READING TIP

Different typeface in a text — for example, **bold** letters or letters in *italics* — means the words have special importance. In this text, bold words are used to indicate the main points about the characteristics of a hero.

Adapted from *Psychology Today.*

Predicting

Before you read

Look at the headings on the opposite page. Then write each heading next to the sentence you think comes from that section.

1. A true hero demonstrates kindness to others. *Kindness, love, and generosity*
2. Heroes must win our hearts as well as our minds. ______
3. Whatever heroes are, they aren't cowards or quitters. ______
4. Heroes are willing to place themselves in some sort of danger. ______
5. A hero's success comes from his or her talents. ______
6. Deception violates the concept of heroism. ______

Skimming

Reading

Skim the text to check your predictions. Then read the whole text.

Guessing meaning from context

After you read

A **Find the words in *italics* in the reading. Circle the meaning of each word.**

1. When you have *potential*, you have the **fear** / **knowledge** / (**possibility**) of becoming something. (par. 1)
2. When you *nurture* something, you **develop** / **question** / **stop** it. (par. 2)
3. When you *maintain composure*, you **are cool and calm under pressure** / **behave in a friendly way** / **have a pleasant appearance**. (par. 3)
4. A *foe* is **a stranger** / **an enemy** / **a relative**. (par. 5)
5. When you *attribute* an action to something, you **accept** / **deny** / **credit** it. (par. 6)

Making inferences

B **Check (✓) the statements that are true.**

✓ 1. Anyone can be a hero.
___ 2. All heroes possess courage, strength, and honesty.
___ 3. Courage and strength are the most important qualities of a hero.
___ 4. Children need to have heroes.
___ 5. Schools can develop heroic qualities in children by encouraging them to develop certain character traits.

Relating reading to personal experience

C **Answer these questions.**

1. Do you agree that the world today lacks heroes? If so, why do you think this is true? If not, who do you think today's heroes are?
2. Think of someone you consider a hero. Which of the qualities mentioned in the reading does or did this person have?
3. Do you think it is important for school children to learn about the lives of people who changed the world and did great things? Why or why not?

ARE ATHLETES *WORTHY* HEROES?

1 These days, it seems, the sports pages have come to read like the police news. The fan looking for game scores must first read news stories about drug use among athletes and reports of other serious crimes. "What's going on here?" sports fans ask. What's happening to our heroes?

2 It is not difficult to understand our desire for athletes to be heroes. On the surface, at least, athletes display many of the classical qualities of heroes. And sports allow us to witness acts that can truly be described as courageous, thrilling, beautiful, and even noble. In an increasingly complicated world, sports is still an area in which we can regularly witness a certain kind of greatness.

3 Yet there's something strange here. The qualities a society looks for in its heroes — selflessness and social consciousness — are precisely the opposite of those needed to become a successful athlete. Becoming a star athlete requires extreme self-absorption, extraordinary physical skills, and a very competitive personality. These qualities may make a great athlete, but they don't necessarily make a great person. Moreover, our society reinforces these qualities with the system it has created to produce athletes — a system that gives athletes the sense they are stars who can do whatever they want.

4 Young athletes learn that success, rather than hard and honest play, is what brings rewards. And for those successful enough to rise to big-time college sports, the "reward" is often an artificially controlled social environment that frees them from many of the responsibilities other students face. Coaches — whose own jobs depend on maintaining winning sports programs — watch over their athletes to make sure that nothing threatens their ability to compete. If an athlete gets into trouble with the police, for instance, a coach will probably try to take care of things. In some schools, athletes don't even choose their own classes or buy their own books; the coach does it all.

5 Given this situation, it's not too surprising that many young American athletes seem to think of themselves as special or even privileged people, and it grows worse the longer they participate in athletics. Universities take care of their every need. Communities look to them as heroes. The public thinks of them as stars. They're paid tremendous amounts of money. And they begin to think they deserve it all.

6 Needless to say, not all athletes are like this. There are plenty of athletes who want to help others. After retiring from football, Alan Page became a successful lawyer and established the Page Education Foundation, which helps young people around the country pay for college. Thankfully, there will always be some true heroes to be found among professional athletes.

7 Still, it's probably misguided for society to look to athletes for its heroes — any more than to look to actors or lawyers. The social role played by athletes is indeed important, but it's different from that of heroes.

Adapted from *Utne Reader.*

Before you read

Relating to the topic

Check (✔) the statements you agree with.

_____ 1. We can witness a certain kind of greatness in sports.
_____ 2. The qualities of heroes and of athletes are exactly the opposite.
_____ 3. Success, not hard and honest play, brings rewards.
_____ 4. There are plenty of athletes who want to help others.
_____ 5. Society should look to athletes for its heroes.

Reading

Scanning

Scan the text and check (✔) the statements the writer agrees with. Then read the whole text.

After you read

Understanding main ideas

A Write the letter of the main idea of each paragraph.

__b__ 1. Paragraph 1 a. Sports fans aren't happy with their athletes.
b. Athletes get into a lot of trouble with the police.
_____ 2. Paragraph 2 a. Athletes and heroes have some qualities in common.
b. People want their athletes to be heroes.
_____ 3. Paragraph 3 a. Athletes and heroes do not have the same qualities.
b. Athletes need to be competitive, but heroes do not.
_____ 4. Paragraph 4 a. The only responsibility athletes have is to be successful.
b. Coaches take care of everything for young athletes.
_____ 5. Paragraph 5 a. Everybody thinks athletes are more special than others.
b. Athletes think they are more important than others.
_____ 6. Paragraph 6 a. Alan Page helps youths.
b. Some athletes are heroes.
_____ 7. Paragraph 7 a. It's not good for society to see its athletes as heroes.
b. Athletes and heroes have important roles in society.

Restating

B Compare the meaning of each pair of sentences. Write same (*S*) or different (*D*).

__D__ 1. On the surface, athletes display many of the qualities of heroes.
In reality, athletes exhibit a lot of heroic behavior.
_____ 2. Society reinforces these qualities with its system of producing athletes.
The public supports the traits of athletes and how they are chosen.
_____ 3. Needless to say, not all athletes are like this.
Of course, this is not true about all athletes.
_____ 4. It's misguided for society to look to athletes for its heroes.
It's ill-advised to expect athletes to be heroes.
_____ 5. The social role of athletes is important, but it's different from that of heroes.
Athletes perform a more valuable function in society than heroes.

Relating reading to personal experience

C Answer these questions.

1. How are athletes in your society treated?
2. How would you describe your favorite athletes?
3. What social role do athletes play in your society?

The hero of my life

1 The man who opened the door that day is the hero of my life. How do I say this without sounding sappy? Blurt it out — the man saved me. He offered exactly what I needed, without questions, without any words at all. He took me in. He was there at the critical time — a silent, watchful presence. Six days later, when it ended, I was unable to find a proper way to thank him, wand I never have. And so, if nothing else, this story represents a small gesture of gratitude 20 years overdue.

2 Even after two decades, I can close my eyes and return to that porch at the Tip Top Lodge. I can see the old guy staring at me. Elroy Berdahl: 81 years old, skinny and shrunken and mostly bald. He wore a flannel shirt and brown work pants. . . . His eyes had the bluish gray color of a razor blade, the same polished shine, and as he peered up at me, I felt a strange sharpness, almost painful, a cutting sensation, as if his gaze were somehow slicing me open. In part, no doubt, it was my own sense of guilt, but even so, I'm absolutely certain that the old man took one look and went right to the heart of things — a kid in trouble. When I asked for a room, Elroy made a little clicking sound with his tongue. He nodded, led me out to one of the cabins, and dropped a key in my hand. . . .

3 "Dinner at five-thirty," he said. "You eat fish?"

4 "Anything," I said.

5 Elroy grunted and said, "I'll bet."

6 We spent six days together at the Tip Top Lodge. Just the two of us . . . Over those six days Elroy Berdahl and I took most of our meals together. In the mornings we sometimes went out on long hikes into the woods, and at night we played Scrabble or listened to records or sat reading in front of his big stone fireplace. At times I felt the awkwardness of an intruder, but Elroy accepted me into his quiet routine without fuss or ceremony. He took my presence for granted, the same way he might've sheltered a stray cat — no wasted sighs or pity — and there was never any talk about it. Just the opposite. What I remember more than anything is the man's willful, almost ferocious silence. In all that time together, all those hours, he never asked the obvious questions: Why was I there? Why alone? Why so preoccupied? If Elroy was curious about any of this, he was careful never to put it into words. . . .

7 The man's self-control was amazing. He never pried. He never put me in a position that required lies or denials . . . Simple politeness was part of it. But even more than that, I think, the man understood that words were insufficient. The problem had gone beyond discussion.

Adapted from *The Things They Carried.*

Thinking about personal experience

Before you read

Check (✔) the ways you think another person could help you with a personal problem.

____ 1. ask you a lot of questions about the problem
____ 2. try to get you to talk about the problem
____ 3. spend a lot of time with you
____ 4. try to get you to talk to others about the problem
____ 5. let you work out the problem by yourself

Skimming

Reading

Skim the text to find out how the narrator's hero helped him. Then read the whole text.

After you read

Recognizing sources

A The text is from a book. What do you think it is about? Check (✔) the correct answer.

____ 1. a man's memories of growing up very poor with his mother and sister
____ 2. family problems and the ways people try to improve their realtionships
____ 3. the difficulties people live with and how they learn from these problems

Guessing meaning from context

B Find the words in *italics* in the reading. Then match each word with its meaning.

c 1. *sappy* (par. 1)	a. uninvited guest
____ 2. *critical* (par. 1)	b. very important
____ 3. *intruder* (par. 6)	c. very emotional
____ 4. *without fuss* (par. 6)	d. not enough
____ 5. *ferocious* (par. 6)	e. strong
____ 6. *insufficient* (par. 7)	f. in an informal way

Making inferences

C Check (✔) the statements that are true.

✓ 1. Elroy lived alone.
____ 2. The narrator and Elroy never saw each other again after the days at the lodge.
____ 3. Elroy had a grandson the same age as the narrator.
____ 4. During his lifetime, Elroy had known many people with problems.
____ 5. When the narrator left the lodge, he knew what to do about his problem.
____ 6. Elroy was upset that the narrator never thanked him for his help.

Relating reading to personal experience

D Answer these questions.

1. Do you think that Elroy's response was the best way to help the narrator? Would it have helped you? What else could he have done?
2. What do you think the narrator's problem was when he arrived at the lodge?
3. What would you do if a friend came to you with a personal problem? What about a stranger?

Vocabulary expansion

A **Complete the chart. Use the words from the box below and the suffixes *-ity*, *-ness*, and *-ship*. Then add your own word to each column.**

Nouns ending in *–ity*	Nouns ending in *–ness*	Nouns ending in *–ship*
ability	*awareness*	*companionship*

~~able~~	conscious	generous	member	popular
~~aware~~	equal	happy	nervous	relation
awkward	friend	kind	noble	sad
~~companion~~	friendly	leader	original	secure

B **Complete the questions with nouns from exercise A. Then answer the questions. (Note: In some cases, more than one noun is correct.)**

1. Who in the class has a lot of *responsibilities* ?
2. Who in the class shows ________________ skills?
3. Who in the class is known for his or her ________________ to others?
4. With whom in the class have you developed a ________________ ?
5. Who in the class shows ________________ in the clothes he or she wears?
6. Who in the class has the ________________ to speak English well?

Heroes and you

It is well-known that firefighters, police officers, and soldiers often perform heroic acts in their working lives. But what about people who do less dangerous work? Work in pairs. Think of ways in which the people below could be heroes at work.

bus drivers	farmers	mail carriers	nurses	reporters
dentists	fisherman	musicians	politicians	teachers

Acknowledgments

Illustration credits

Matt Collins	**4, 20, 61, 87**
Ray Alma	**6, 14, 36, 74, 115**
William Waitzman	**11, 18, 59, 112, 126**
Adam Hurwitz	**8, 16, 118**
David Rolfe	**46, 92**
Daniel Vasconcellos	**50, 90, 94**
Bob Burnett	**66, 71**

Photographic credits

2 Markowitz Jeffrey/Corbis Sygma
12 Courtesy of Electronic Arts
22 Bettmann/Corbis
26 Bettmann/Corbis
28 Getty Images
29 (*clockwise from top left*) Terry Vine/Getty Images; Cat Gwynn/Getty Images; Reza Estakhrian/Getty Images; Aneal Vohra/Unicorn Photos; Getty Images; Chris Windsor/Getty Images;
30 Courtesy of Helping Hands
34 Neal Preston/Corbis
38 Courtesy of Warner Brothers
42 Robert Dowling/Corbis
44 Marc Romanelli/Getty Images
52 Ariel Skelley/Corbis
54 Photofest
58 V.C.L./Getty Images
60 Yang Liu/Corbis
62 Trinette Reed/Corbis
68 Michael Keller/Corbis
70 Ghislain & Marie David de Lossy/Getty Images
76 (*top to bottom*) David Turnley/Corbis; Getty Images; Creatas
78 Photofest
82 Bettmann/Corbis
84 (*bottom right*) Gary Randall/Getty Images; all others Photodisc
98 Corbis
100 Courtesy of *The Daily Telegraph*
102 Paul & Lindamarie Ambrose/Getty Images
106 AP/Wide World Photos
108 Anna CLopet/Corbis
110 Lester Lefkowitz/Corbis
114 Courtesy of Edy's Ice Cream
116 David Stoecklein/Corbis
122 Nogues Alain/Corbis
124 Reuters NewMedia Inc./Corbis

Text credits

The authors and publishers are grateful for permission to reprint the following items:

2 Adapted from *Multicultural Manners*, by Norine Dresser. Copyright © 1996. This material is used by permission of John Wiley & Sons, Inc.

4 Adapted from "A Sense of Identity. Do Folks Like Their First Names? Most Do—Or Eventually Will," by Mary Lynn Plageman, *The Columbus Dispatch*, April 4, 1999, page 1D.

6 Adapted from "Keep Maiden Name, Readers Tell Bride," Ann Landers' column, *The Toronto Star*, December 9, 1999. By permission of Ann Landers and Creators Syndicate, Inc.

10 Adapted from *Games for Rains, Planes, and Trains*, by Gyles Brandreth. The Stephen Greene Press, Brattleboro, Vermont 05301 © 1974 by Gyles Brandreth, pages 27, 34, 64, and 73.

12 Adapted from "The Majestic Matrix; Intrusive Online Game May Start New Genre," by Kelly Zito, *The San Francisco Chronicle*, April 9, 2001, page B1.

14 Adapted from "Women playing games," by Nick Jankel-Elliott, *Financial Times* (London), November 28, 2000, Survey – Creative Business section, page 16. Copyright © 2000 The Financial Times Limited.

18 Adapted from "Fun Steps to Fitness," by Amanda Gardner and Lola Ogunnaike, *Daily News* (New York), November 1, 1999, page 38. Copyright © 1999 Daily News, L.P.

20 Adapted from "Oriental Dance: A Dance For The Whole Family," by Shira. From the website http://www.shira.net/whole-family.htm.

22 Adapted from *How to Enjoy Ballet*, by Mary Clarke and Clement Crisp, pages 12, 13, and 16. Copyright © 1983 by Judy Piatkus Publishers Limited of Loughton, Essex.

26 Adapted from "If you see someone in trouble, don't just stand there," by Kristine Larsen, *Glamour*, Vol. 91, Issue 12, December 1993, page 91.
Adapted from "Why good people don't help," by Harriet Brown, *McCall's*, July 1993, pages 82-84 and 136.

28 Adapted from "Practise Random Kindness And Senseless Acts of Beauty" from the website http://www.globalideasbank.org/BOV/BV-82.HTML.

30 Adapted from "'Guide Dog' to Paralyzed Aide Monkeys A Saving Grace," by K.C. Baker, *Daily News* (New York), October 10, 1998, page 22. Copyright © 1998 Daily News, L.P.

34 Adapted from "School of hard knocks Toronto stunt school teaches safe 'crash' courses," by Peter Cheney, *The Toronto Star*, January 14, 1989, page H1. Reprinted with permission – The Toronto Star Syndicate. From an article originally appearing in the The Toronto Star, January 1989. Copyright © 1989 Toronto Star Newspapers, Ltd.

36 Adapted from "Companies in the high-pressure extra business learn to meet unusual requests in short order," by Valerie Hauch, *The Toronto Star*, April 21, 1997, page C1. Copyright Valerie Hauch. Reprinted with permission – The Toronto Star Syndicate. From an article originally appearing in The Toronto Star, April 1997.

38 Adapted from "The Storyteller," by Ronald Grover, *Business Week*, July 13, 1998, page 96, Copyright © 1998 The McGraw-Hill Companies, Inc.

42 Adapted from "Living with mother," by Teresa Poole, *The Independent*, May 27, 1994, page 7.

44 Adapted from "[his]," by Michael Dorris, *Glamour*, June 1994, page 226. (Adapted from *Paper Trail*) Copyright © 1994 HarperCollins Publishers Inc.

46 From THE FUTURE OF SUCCESS, by Robert B. Reich, Copyright © 2000 by Robert B. Reich. Used by permission of Alfred A. Knopf, a division of Random House, Inc.

50 Pages 138-139 from MEN ARE FROM MARS, WOMEN ARE FROM VENUS by John Gray Copyright © 1992 by John Gray. Reprinted by permission of HarperCollins Publishers Inc.

52 Adapted from "Men, Women, and Sports: Audience Experiences and Effects," by W. Ganz and L.A. Wenner, *Journal of Broadcasting & Electronic Media*, Spring 91, Vol. 35, Issue 2, page 233. The reprint permission is granted to use this BEA publication (Journal of Broadcasting & Electronic Media) from the Broadcast Education Association, www.beaewb.org.
Adapted from "One Game, Two Arenas," *Psychology Today*, Sep 92, Vol. 25, Issue 5, page 13.

54 From *Barefoot In The Park*, by Neil Simon, pages 94-96. Copyright © by Ellen Enterprises, 1964. Reprinted by permission of William Morris Agency, Inc. on behalf of the Author.

58 Adapted from "Tactics for Spotting Communication Problems," by Joanne Cole, *Take Charge Assistant*, May 1, 1997, Vol. 3. Copyright © 1997 American Management Association.

60 Adapted from "Who says babies can't talk?" by Linda Acredolo and Susan Goodwyn, *Parents*, S'96, Vol. 71, pages 86-8+.

62 Adapted from "Essay: Mind Your Language," by Justin Webster, *The Independent*, March 4, 2000, pages 31, 33, 34, 35. Adapted extracts from an article by Justin Webster first published in The Independent 4 March 2000.

66 Adapted from "A Fish Story, or Not?" by Joseph T. Wells, *Journal of Accountancy*, November 2001. Copyright © 2001 from the Journal of Accountancy by the American Institute of Certified Public Accountants, Inc. Opinions of the authors are their own and do not necessarily reflect the policies of the AICPA. Reprinted with permission.

68 Adapted from "When advertising claims sound false // Ad industry whistle-blowers often sound alarm," by Anthony Giorgianni, *Minneapolis Star Tribune*, November 10, 1996, page 14E.

70 "Truth or Consequences" David Oliver Relin published in THE NEW YORK TIMES UPFRONT, January 1, 2001. Copyright © 2001 by The New York Times Company. Reprinted by permission of Scholastic Inc.

74 Adapted from "Cellphone yakkers should clam up: People discussing private business in public need lessons in manners," by Patricia Horn, *The Ottawa Citizen*, May 8, 2000, page B12. Copyright © 2000 CanWest Interactive.

76 Adapted from "How table manners became polite," by Sharon J. Huntington, reprinted from *The Christian Science Monitor*, November 28, 2000, page 22.

78 From *The Joy Luck Club* by Amy Tan, pages 196-199. Copyright 1990 by Putnam Publishing Group.

82 Adapted from "True love is all over in 30 months," by John Harlow, *The Sunday Times.* Copyright © Times Newspapers Limited, London (July 25, 1999).

84 Adapted from "What dogs, mates have in common," by Vicki Crocke, *The Boston Globe*, March 20, 1999, page F1. Copyright © 1999 Globe Newspaper Company.
86 Love Song for Lucinda, by Langston Hughes
Ashes of Life, by Edna St. Vincent Millay
90 Adapted from "Flying? No fear," by Stephen Bleach, *The Sunday Times*. Copyright © Stephen Bleach/Times Newspapers Limited, London (December 31, 2000).
92 Adapted from "Don't fight a good fright; Halloween scares are fun, but living with real phobias can be a nightmare," by Gary Rotstein, *Pittsburgh Post-Gazette*, October 31, 2000, page F-1. Copyright © *Pittsburgh Post-Gazette*, 2002 All rights reserved. Reprinted with permission.
94 Adapted from "Classical Music; Taking Arms Against Stage Fright," by Eleanor Blau, *The New York Times*, September 20, 1998, page 33. Copyright © 1998 by the New York Times Co. Reprinted by permission.
98 Adapted from "In Britain: Schools use hypnosis to combat stress," by Alfred Lee, *The Straits Times* (Singapore), October 18, 2000, page 6.
100 Adapted from "Psychic reveals secrets of her 22-year career cracking crime," by Tim Reid, *Sunday Telegraph*, June 23, 1996, page 3. Copyright © 1996 The Telegraph Group Limited.
102 Adapted from "What is a Near-Death Experience (NDE)?" from the website http://www.iands.org/nde.html. Copyright © 1996-2002 by IANDS.
106 Adapted from "The day a language died," by Peter Popham, *The Independent*, January 20, 1996.
108 Adapted from "Aping Language," by Sharon Begley, From *Newsweek*, January 19, 1998 © 1998 Newsweek, Inc. All rights reserved. Reprinted by permission.
110 Adapted from "The Bilingual Brain," *Discover*, Vol.18, October 1997, page 26. Reprinted by permission from the October 1997 issue of Discover Magazine.
114 Adapted from "Ice Cream Taste-Tester Has Sweetest Job in America," by Sylvia Rector, *The Times-Picayune*, September 11, 1998, page L32. Copyright © 1998 The Times-Picayune Publishing Co.
116 Adapted from "A Primer on Smell," by Elise Hancock. From the website www.jhu.edu/~jhumag/996web/smell.html. Reprinted with the permission of Johns Hopkins Magazine.
118 Adapted from "How deafness makes it easier to hear In Sickness and Health," by Dr. James Le Fanu, *Sunday Telegraph*, August 11, 1996, page 4. Copyright © 1996 The Telegraph Group Limited.
122 Adapted from "How to be great! What does it take to be a hero? Start with six basic character traits," *Psychology Today*, Vol. 28, November 21, 1995, page 46. REPRINTED WITH PERMISSION FROM PSYCHOLOGY TODAY MAGAZINE, Copyright © (1995 Sussex Publishers, Inc.).
124 Adapted from "Where have you gone, Joe DiMaggio?" by Matthew Goodman. Reprinted with permission from *Utne Reader* May/June 1993. To subscribe, call 800/736-UTNE or visit our Web site at www.utne.com.
126 Excerpt from "On the Rainy River," from THE THINGS THEY CARRIED by Tim O'Brien. Copyright © 1990 by Tim O'Brien. Reprinted by permission of Houghton Mifflin Company. All rights reserved.

Every effort has been made to trace the owners of copyright material in this book. We would be grateful to hear from anyone who recognizes their copyright material and who is unacknowledged. We will be pleased to make the necessary corrections in future editions of the book.